Fit to Pitch

Tom House, PhD
Pitching Coach and Consultant

Human Kinetics

Library of Congress Cataloging-in-Publication Data

House, Tom, 1947–
    Fit to pitch / Tom House.
      p. cm.
    Includes index.
    ISBN 0-87322-882-0
    1. Pitching (Baseball)   2. Pitchers (Baseball)--Training of.
  I. Title.
  GV871.H5 1996
  796.357'22--dc20   95-44482
                                            CIP

ISBN: 0-87322-882-0

Developmental Editor: Rodd Whelpley; **Assistant Editor:** Kent Reel; **Editorial Assistant:** Jennifer Hemphill; **Copyeditor:** Bob Replinger; **Proofreader:** Pam Johnson; **Indexer:** Theresa Schaefer; **Typesetter:** Francine Hamerski; **Layout Artists:** Robert Reuther and Francine Hamerski; **Text Designer:** Robert Reuther; **Photo Editor:** Boyd LaFoon; **Cover Designer:** Jack Davis; **Photographer (cover):** Courtesy of University of Oklahoma; **Photographers (interior):** Cheyenne Rouse and Wilmer Zehr; **Illustrator:** Studio 2-D; **Printer:** Edwards Bros.

Printed in the United States of America   10 9 8 7 6 5 4 3 2 1

Human Kinetics
Web site: http://www.humankinetics.com

United States: Human Kinetics
P.O. Box 5076, Champaign, IL 61825-5076
1-800-747-4457

Canada: Human Kinetics, Box 24040, Windsor, ON N8Y 4Y9
1-800-465-7301 (in Canada only)

Europe: Human Kinetics, P.O. Box IW14, Leeds LS16 6TR, United Kingdom
(44) 1132 781708

Australia: Human Kinetics, 57A Price Avenue, Lower Mitcham, South Australia
(08) 371 3755

New Zealand: Human Kinetics, P.O. Box 105-231, Auckland 1
(09) 523 3462

Contents

Foreword

A pitching career is a fragile thing, and sometimes it is easy to lose sight of that. Coaches often get caught up in the winning and losing and fail to consider the long-term health concerns of their athlete. Even at the professional level, some players don't really appreciate how soon a career can end—and careers have ended prematurely—for too many pitchers.

Tom House has seen a lot of promising pitching careers ruined by poor pitching mechanics, and even more cut short by poor training habits. He's been a crusader on both topics. His emphasis on functional fitness addresses mechanics and training strategy. No wasted movement and no wasted time, transferring benefits gained in the training room to the pitching mound.

In *Fit to Pitch* you're getting state-of-the-art and science conditioning ideas for a successful, long pitching career. You'll find effective and efficient pitcher-specific exercises, drills, workouts, and programs, and you'll get insights—such as when a sore arm is an injured arm—that will help get you healthy, if necessary, and will keep you healthy.

Some say I'm an imposing figure on the mound. Perhaps so. But my 95+ mph fastball is only going to intimidate hitters if I refine my mechanics and keep myself in top shape.

Use the information in *Fit to Pitch* and make the most out of your pitching potential. You just may be surprised at how much potential you have!

Randy Johnson
Seattle Mariners

Preface

The pitcher. No other position in sports is as crucial to a team's success. Some claim that pitching is 90 percent of the game. Whatever the actual percentage, it's far too important for modern pitchers to rely on outdated training methods. Until recently, it has been difficult to objectively identify proper mechanics and physical conditioning for pitchers. Even now, as I travel around the world advising pitchers and coaches, I get questions like these:

- Should a pitcher develop his arm or his entire body?
- Does in-season weight lifting cause control problems?
- How many pitches should a pitcher throw in an inning? a game? a week?
- If I weight train, will I throw harder?
- Are heavy weights bad for a pitcher?

Fit to Pitch answers these and other questions about what it takes to prepare for the physical demands of pitching. The book explains and illustrates preventive conditioning (prehab) guidelines, exercises, and programs to maximize pitching performance and minimize the risk of injury. Another important part of the book addresses rehabilitative conditioning that a pitcher needs to do to return to competition after an injury.

The information included in these chapters synthesizes the best of contemporary sport science, modern medical science, and practical baseball experience. The training protocols are weight-room and field tested by American, Latin, and Japanese pitchers of all ages, abilities, skill levels, and conditioning levels in rehab and prehab assignments. The suggested programs combine the best of the old with the best of the new. In the past, most experts agreed on what a pitcher should do to get his body in shape. The current issues have been how pitchers should train their bodies, arms, *and* pitching mechanics. What programs will best accomplish the things everyone wants—to build up a pitcher's body and arm and to match this strength with an efficient delivery so he can perform at his peak and stay healthy?

Some components of my protocols challenge traditional thought. You will learn why pitchers should throw with their elbows up (in what I call the *Flex-T*) for good mechanics. You will see an emphasis on postural stabilization with work on elbow and shoulder joint integrity both in the weight room and on the field. You will learn why "integrated flexibility" with joint, connective tissue, and muscle is a better approach for stabilization than the traditional "stretching out" of an elbow or shoulder. You will learn why tired arm, or overuse syndrome, has caused pitchers problems for 125 years. The cause is self-evident: too much throwing off a mound. The prevention comes from new information about how teaching skill work on flat ground will push back the wall of fatigue most pitchers experience during the course of a season. You will also learn how matching throwing workloads with training workloads will facilitate recovery time and help a pitcher peak in competition.

For the last few years I have worked around the world with field personnel, as well as with medical and conditioning staffs. The net result has been the development of a comprehensive conditioning program for pitchers that

1. maximizes performance,
2. minimizes risk of injury, and
3. promotes improved conditioning and performance after injury.

In *Fit to Pitch*, you will find answers to many questions a coach, a pitcher, or a concerned parent has about pitching and training to pitch. I've organized the book into three parts. In part I, Fit to Pitch Training Components, you will find illustrations and explanations of how flexibility and strength-training exercises are performed. You will also discover how pitchers can build up—and not tear down—the arm when they practice throwing. In part II, Fit to Pitch Training Program, I show you how to set up training programs, including daily resistance workouts, throwing sessions for between-game appearances, and a season-long plan. You will learn what adjustments are needed depending on age, level of fitness, and ability. Throughout the book, you will find little tips that can make a big difference in helping a pitcher stay injury free. If injuries occur, part III, Fit to Pitch Rehab and Nutrition, is useful since it addresses being hurt and provides rehabilitative protocols for the many pathologies pitchers experience. You will learn that it *is* possible to bounce back from injury.

This book takes the guesswork out of how to get fit for pitching. Whether you are a pitcher who is using the information as a training manual, or a coach or parent using it as a tool to advise pitchers, you will appreciate how the specific physical and mechanical preparation recommended in *Fit to Pitch* transfers to game performance. When a pitcher develops functional strength, he is able to use more efficient mechanics through the pitching motion and ultimately feels more confident about his ability to perform. When training, technique, and thinking are properly integrated, the pitcher will increase his chances to be successful and healthy.

Part I

Fit to Pitch Training Components

Chapters 1 through 7 give the reader a synthesis of clinical research and practical experience from today's contemporary baseball environment. It's important to realize just how global this knowledge base is. There isn't a pitching book in the game today with a better grasp of the traditions and teachings that created the unorthodox delivery of Hideo Nomo or the objective information and instruction that gave focus to the overpowering talent of Randy Johnson.

The components of *Fit to Pitch* will help explain why every pitcher looks different doing the same things to throw a baseball and how every pitcher can individualize his physical and mechanical preparation for more competitive success and less risk of injury.

Chapter 1, Training to Pitch, is an overview of physical and mechanical training principles. Goals and objectives from sports medicine are integrated with goals and objectives from on-the-field instruction. Some new vocabulary is defined to better explain how *cross-specificity* enhances the development of skill to support genetic talent.

Chapters 2 through 7 identify and sequence proper training protocols. Each chapter diagnoses, defines, and describes a proper exercise component and shows how to integrate it into a pitcher's total fitness.

Chapter 1

Training to Pitch

I ain't ever had a job, I always just played baseball.

—Satchel Paige

Ol' Satch played in a different era. Today ballplayers still play the game, but it is a job. And the first part of the job, a job that can yield significant rewards, is training to compete. The goal when training to pitch is for an athlete to match his body's most efficient delivery (his mechanics) with a functional strength base (his physical condition) to handle the number of times he must deliver a baseball per inning, per game, per season (his throwing workloads).

Everyone agrees that pitching mechanics, conditioning, and workload are the key factors in maintaining a healthy arm. Sports medicine specialists take it a step further, pointing out that a pitcher's body has three primary lines of defense for the physical wear and tear of throwing a baseball:

1. Muscle tissue
2. Connective tissue
3. Bone tissue

In other words, if a pitcher gets tendinitis, his muscles weren't strong enough to handle either the number of pitches he was throwing or the mechanics of his delivery. If a pitcher gets spurs, bone chips, or stress fractures, then the muscles and connective tissues were underdeveloped for his throwing workloads and delivery mechanics over the course of many games, a season, or a career.

It makes sense, then, for a pitcher to have training goals in mind before he considers any performance goals, because haphazard or improper training can lead to subpar performance or injury.

Training Goals

When conditioning or rehabilitating, find a proper balance between strength building and pitching workloads. Both components are functions of volume, load, frequency, intensity, and duration. Add a third component, proper throwing mechanics, and you have what it takes to build and protect the muscle tissues, connective tissues, and bone tissues that make up healthy arms.

A fourth component—the human mind—can be equally important. If a pitcher has problems on the mental or emotional side, developing the body will take him only so far. Nolan Ryan pitched for a quarter century in the major leagues because he followed many of the exercise prescriptions presented in this book *and* he worked on psychological skills. Greg Maddux and Randy Johnson achieved their high levels of performance and complete-game stamina with a combination of hard and smart training, the kind of programs emphasized in this book. They take their physical and mental preparation very seriously, because they know what will happen if they don't. It's also a fact that many injured pitchers have made tremendous comebacks from injuries by combining the appropriate rehabilitative regimen (see chapter 10) with a positive and aggressive mental approach.

Physical preparation for pitching is multidimensional. While strength is an asset, so is flexibility. And neither of those will do you any good in the late innings if you lack sufficient stamina. To be effective, then, a pitcher fitness program must integrate several training components.

Training Variables Quantified

Conditioning coaches and trainers can quantify and control pitching workloads by using these variables: volume, load, frequency, intensity, and duration.

Volume

How many pitches did you throw during your last practice? Inning? Game? Volume refers to the total number of pitches in a time frame or the total amount of resistance training in a time frame. You need to quantify your training workload for a given period, and that training workload should match your typical pitching workload for the same time frame. I've found one-week increments work best when integrating throwing and strength-training programs. For example, in one week a starting pitcher's mound volume would equal the cumulative stress generated by the number of pregame and game pitches plus the number of bullpen pitches thrown between starts. In that same week, a starting pitcher's training volume would equal the sum of all his resistance work.

Load

The resistance or load experienced by the pitcher's body on every pitch is a function of velocity and mechanical efficiency. A pitcher with good velocity and bad mechanics works harder than a pitcher with good velocity and good mechanics. That's why pitchers with better mechanics tend to last longer than pitchers who throw at the same speed but have mechanical flaws in their delivery. I'll explain the formula for determining load in chapter 9. At this point, remember that smart conditioning requires you to match your training loads and your pitching loads. Proper strength training is skill-specific in position, movement, and resistance. Skill training occurs in the weight room *and* on the field. This cross-specific protocol teaches you efficiency—delivering the ball with the minimal amount of work to yield the desired result.

Frequency

Frequency is the total number of mound sessions in a given time frame. For example, a short reliever or closer will usually appear in three to five games per week, but it is not unusual for him to warm up (a "scare" in baseball terms) six to seven times per week. In a busy week, short relievers may throw as much as a starter! Proper resistance training will break volumes into lifting sessions equal to the frequency of mound sessions. Ideally, this will physically prepare each pitcher to be able to answer the call as often as it comes for as long as his services are required.

Intensity

How much effort does each pitch take and how close together do the pitches follow each other in a workout session? Effort, in this case, is a measure of the intensity of work. Throwing 30 successive pitches at 100 percent effort is far more intense than two sets of 15 pitches at 80 percent effort with a 30- to 60-second pause between sets.

I will say it here and in later chapters: Skill training is low-intensity work. Strive for perfection at a level of effort that feels good. Game work is high-intensity work, where the objective is to get hitters out with whatever effort it takes. So, let your conditioning train your body for the highly intense work of game-day pitching. Use your skill training to work on mechanical efficiency (which, incidentally, reduces the effort it will take to deliver those high-intensity pitches).

Duration

Duration is the amount of time spent per session. Starting pitchers are on the mound much longer, per game, than relievers. So the starting staff must be trained, on and off the field, to be durable over a long outing with ample recovery time. Relievers must be trained, on and off the field, for less durability but quicker recovery.

Smart Training

By measuring throwing volume, load, frequency, intensity, and duration, you can determine a baseline for the amount of resistance volume, load, frequency, and intensity you should be doing per week. You can manipulate the throwing training variables in a number of ways and, ultimately, your resistance-training protocols. For example, use these approaches to vary your training:

- Use flat-ground instead of mound throwing to reduce intensity and load.
- Set limits on the number of pitches thrown during a session to control duration.
- Vary load and intensity by using short, medium, or long toss in combination with a sequencing of bullpen skill work, batting practice, or simulated games.

Keep in mind that starters, with large pitch counts and fewer outings, will have much different pitching volume and frequency than relievers, who have lower pitch counts but many outings.

By manipulating both throwing and resistance-training variables you'll be able to do more than simply track pitching workloads, although that is important. The real payoff is that you'll have more options to develop training programs that meet your specific needs. I'll present several sample training programs in chapter 9 for you to consider.

Remember also that there's another facet of smart training to explore. And that's specificity training. In addition to tailoring entire programs to match the workloads required for certain types of pitchers, the components of those training programs—stretches, exercises, and drills—can be designed so that pitchers train their muscles and connective tissues in the same way they will be used when they support the body as it moves through an efficient pitching motion.

The Pitching Motion

Fit to Pitch is not intended to be a primer on pitching efficiency. However, since the stretches and exercises presented in this book are specifically designed to prepare your body to withstand the stresses a proper pitching motion requires, let's review the basics of proper pitching mechanics.

Throwing starts with the feet and proceeds through legs, torso, arms, and finally the baseball. At some point in both the windup and the stretch, a pitcher must find a dynamically balanced position with weight evenly distributed between the balls of the feet, with knees slightly flexed, and in a comfortable, stable posture (which is roughly analogous to a proper batting stance). His head is over and slightly in front of his center of gravity (the belly button), and he will hold his head steady throughout the pitching motion so as not to lose balance.

The pitcher will then create a weight shift (and load his kinetic energy system) by lifting the front leg, with the knee toward the center of gravity to absorb energy over the ball of the foot on his posting, or back, leg (see figure 1.1). He will then stride forward toward the plate in a ball-of-foot to ball-of-foot

Figure 1.1   Move from (a) the loaded position, to (b) the front strike and the Flex-T, into (c) the late rotation and launch.

direction, separating hand, baseball, and glove from position on line with the center of gravity. Forearm path and angle are unique to each pitcher, but when the front foot hits the mound, his arms will be in what I call the *Flex-T* position with a stable upper-body posture. The Flex-T is a position of optimal joint integrity for shoulders and elbows, where elbows are (1) shoulder-height and slightly in front of the shoulder points, and (2) on line with the hips and balls of the feet. From this stable total body position, the upper body should stay on line in the direction created by striding ball-of-foot to ball-of-foot and rotate as late as possible. The best professional pitchers delay upper-body rotation until their center of gravity has reached at least 75 percent of their stride length. When this finishing rotation is delayed as much as possible, the Flex-T delivers more energy to the throwing forearm, waist, hand, and baseball at a point *closer* to home plate. This is important because releasing the ball one foot closer to home plate seems to add three miles per hour to the speed of the pitch, at least from the hitter's perspective. This is why I tell my pitchers to "stride, glide, and rotate late."

The Pitching Motion and Specificity Training

A pitcher's muscles must have the physical capacity to sequentially load the energy links necessary to throw a baseball efficiently. These energy links start at the feet and finish with the middle finger of the throwing hand. Each link must be able to pass on to the next link its share of the energy created by body weight, stride length, and the slope of the mound. For a pitcher to deliver the baseball efficiently, his mechanics and strength training (the composites of skill) must be able to support his throwing workloads and genetic talent base. So energy created by weight transfer must flow efficiently from posting foot to landing foot, up through the ankles, knees, hips, spine, shoulders, elbows, wrists, and fingers into the baseball. The muscles and connective tissue must be trained to stabilize and balance the bone tissue throughout the pitching motion from the time the pitcher assumes his pitching posture, through his assumption of the Flex-T position, into the late torso rotation, and finally into ball release. Energy cannot be started out of sequence and should not be lost along the way. In the long term, pitchers are only as strong as their weakest link in the energy-transfer system.

Pitching places violent torques and stresses on the entire body, especially the shoulder and elbow. In competition every pitcher will hyperflex and hyperextend his arm as it rotates externally and internally to deliver the baseball. That's a lot of position-specific and movement-specific stress on your energy-transfer system. However, because dynamic balance, postural stabilization, and shoulder-high, Flex-T-positioned elbows are mechanically more efficient, the effects of this stress are considerably diminished. Computerized three-dimensional motion analysis performed at Bio-Kinetics in Salt Lake City, Utah, proves it. So, smart training would suggest that pitchers actually train for dynamic balance, postural stabilization, and joint integrity in an elbows-high, Flex-T position. That's exactly what we'll do in *Fit to Pitch*.

By resistance training to integrate these three biomechanical efficiencies, you are strengthening the neuromuscular "feel" of the most efficient arm and elbow position for delivering the baseball. (Since your body will make proper motion a habit, it only makes sense for your strength training to mirror proper pitching mechanics—right?) Remember, the Flex-T is an optimal strength-training position for a pitcher's shoulder and elbow. It actually promotes joint integrity when cross-training strength and throwing mechanics. It's part of what coaches call "the athletic position" complementing dynamic balance of feet, knees, and hips as well as postural and trunk stabilization created by the spine. Training in the Flex-T reinforces neuromuscular strength and kinesthetic awareness. Think of it as an insurance policy for the shoulder and elbow to resist the negative effects of long-term hyperextension and hyperflexion caused by pitching off a mound. For these reasons you'll see a lot of high-elbow, Flex-T work prescribed both on the field and in the weight room.

Release Points and Specificity Training

As figure 1.2 demonstrates, you mix your pitches by varying your forearm, waist, hand, and ball positions at the release point. In simple baseball terms, if the palm of your hand faces the catcher, you're throwing a fastball. If your palm faces in toward your body, you're throwing a breaking ball. If your palm faces away from your body, it's a change-up.

Since you'll be releasing the ball at the same release point, but with at least three different palm positions, it makes sense to flex and strength train the muscles and connecting tissues in your hands, wrists, forearms, elbow, and shoulders specifically to these positions. That's just what we do in *Fit to Pitch*. Whenever I direct you to flex or perform an arm exercise in a linear position, you should be thinking of the fastball release point. When I direct you to work in a pronate position, assume the change-up position. Strength work in a supinate position is done with the breaking ball release point in mind.

Training Summary

Very few pitchers get by on talent alone. Skill training *and* conditioning are essential for pitching. Proper physical training can reduce the likelihood of joint laxity, hyperflexibility, hyperextension, subluxation, tired arm, impingement, tendinitis, ligamentitus, bursitis, and arthritis. Conversely, pitchers who neglect their training and try to slide by on their talent increase the chances of injury-shortened careers.

A complete training program for pitching combines the proper amount of flexibility work, aerobic and anaerobic conditioning, muscular conditioning, and skill work. The following chapters will show you the basics of these components. First, you'll prepare your body for skill training. Next you'll learn effective skill-training drills, and finally you'll learn how to put these components together in an integrated program to get the most out of your pitching talent.

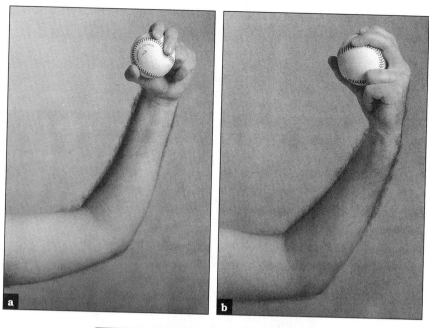

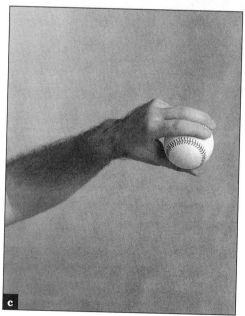

Figure 1.2   The release points: The photos illustrate (a) the linear release point of a fastball, (b) the supinate release point of a breaking ball, and (c) the pronate release point of a change-up.

Flexibility Training

**Stretching the body is like stretching the budget.
Everybody tries it, but nobody really does it.**

Adrian Crook, personal trainer

We all know that stretching—like budgeting—can be benefi-
cial, but you have to do it, and do it correctly, to make it work.
An integrated stretching routine (or flexibility-training routine, as we will call it) should be a part of between-game micro
training cycles and in-season macro training cycles. Flexibility
training is also part of a proper rehabilitation program. In this
chapter I will define the components of a flexibility program
and provide descriptions and illustrations of the flexing tech-
niques for pitchers.

The term *stretching* is really a misnomer. It would be more correct to call the procedure *contracting*. Muscles can get stronger, but not longer, and they contract (rather than stretch) when working properly. Stretching can actually be bad for connective tissue because once stretched out, tendons and ligaments don't bounce back and are never as resilient.

Why Stretch?

At this point you're probably asking yourself, Then why stretch at all? Good question! Here's why: Proper stretching is part of a larger and very desirable goal to integrate nerve, muscle, and connective tissue in a controlled, low-intensity movement. Stretching is actually flexibility training. As you read in the last chapter, smart training tells us that flexibility exercises should be position specific and movement specific. Furthermore, they should balance the total body and be performed only to tolerance, which means simply that you don't stretch your muscles to the point of discomfort. The key concept is controlled activation of the total body to tolerance. In flexibility training you'll use everything the body uses in competition, but you'll go at a submaximal level of intensity.

Athletes should do a total body flex before performing skill work, resistance work, or competing. It's the "pre" part of preparation. A good analogy is the prerace work done to a car in the Indianapolis 500. What happens on race day is the net result of having everything in that car fueled up, touched up, tuned up, and heated up before the starting flag even wiggles. It takes an integrated effort to incorporate everything in precompetition that needs to work at a fantastic clip in competition. Those Indy people work just like smart pitchers!

Integrated Flexibility

This chapter, the longest of the book, provides you with an integrated flexibility workout. The concept is new, the application different, but the rewards are proving to be significant. Let's take a moment to explain what I mean by the word integration. Remember, the human body is only as strong as its weakest link—and that link will reveal itself when stressed daily through its ranges of motion. Training the body for balanced strength and flexibility to meet the demands of this stress is functional integration. Isolation, on the other hand, is working individual muscle groups to create form, not necessarily balance and flexibility. Body builders isolate muscle groups and work to create aesthetically pleasing muscle tissue, not to develop the ability to throw, swing, jump, or run. Unfortunately, a lot of Western physical therapy and weight-training philosophy has revolved around the isolation-based training of body *parts*. Integration training—training body parts in the way they work together—is proving to be far more effective and efficient in the rehab and prehab conditioning of competitive athletes.

I mentioned that this integration idea is new for American baseball. I must give credit to the guy who got me started on body balance and flexibility training, Adrian Crook, a personal trainer who works in southern California. As a balance and flexibility instructor he has westernized much of the oriental mind and body philosophy into practical athletic applications. I have seen his program increase function and performance across the board, whatever the sport, whomever the athlete, and regardless of whether the individual was an elite performer or just someone with everyday ability. But what Adrian has done on a small scale for baseball in the U.S. has been done by trainers and conditioning coaches in Japan. Total body flexibility training, not resistance training, is the primary focus of their off-the-field conditioning. The absolute strength of a typical Japanese pitcher is significantly less than his American counterpart, but the Japanese pitcher will throw two to three times the number of pitches that the American does in a given time frame. All other factors being equal (e.g., velocity, mechanics, stamina, etc.), soft-tissue image research reveals the Japanese athlete's body dissipates the stress of pitching a baseball more efficiently than the American's. The key is integrated flexibility training.

Before getting into the specifics of an integrated flexibility program, I would like to briefly define its critical components. You'll recognize the terms from chapter 1. All the exercises in an integrated flexibility training program are designed to train an athlete's

- dynamic balance,
- trunk stability, and
- joint integrity.

Dynamic Balance

Dynamic balance is controlling the body's center of gravity through weight transfer (i.e., a step, a stride, a lunge, etc.) where in effect, the athlete has absorbed potential energy to direct and deliver kinetic energy into an implement (i.e., a ball, a bat, a racquet, etc.). As a pitcher, when you stride toward the plate, you must control your center of gravity (hence your balance) through your weight transfer. Dynamic balance flexibility exercises prepare your body for this component in the skill of pitching.

Trunk Stabilization

Trunk stabilization could also be called postural stabilization. This is the athlete's ability to maintain, during weight transfer, the angular and linear relationship of head, center of gravity, and balls of feet. For pitchers, like any athlete, the first major joint of stabilization is the ankle, the second is the knee, the third are the hips. Fourth is a whole chain of little joints making up the spine, which then connect to the fifth major joint of stabilization, the shoulder. Sixth is the elbow, seventh is the wrist, and last are the bones of the hand and fingers. Efficient pitching mechanics dictate that your head always be right over your belly button (your center of gravity) when you pitch. If, when you pitch, your head is going in a different direction than the rest of your body, you've got problems (usually proportionate to the speed and distance of the head's misdirection). Mechanical efficiency suffers, muscle and connective tissue must work harder to compensate, performance decreases, and chance of injury increases. Trunk stabilization exercises let your musculoskeletal system practice the postures you'll need on the mound.

Joint Integrity

Joint integrity is a phenomenon achieved when connective tissue and joints interact to bridge muscle and bone. Joints are the levers in and between the torso and limbs that enable energy to be translated from feet to legs, into torso, and out through arms into implements. As I've said before, pitching is really transferring energy through your body to the ball. Your tendons, ligaments, and joints have to be in shape to withstand and support the energy surge generated through your body so that it can be transferred effectively to the baseball.

Sequencing Flexibility Exercises

Flexibility training requires proper sequencing of movements to develop dynamic balance, trunk stabilization, and joint integrity. For training pitchers, the sequential integration for dynamic balance and joint integrity requires working *feet to fingertips* whenever possible. You'll use this sequence because the first sensory signal for pitching balance in movement comes from the balls and arches of your feet. Your brain automatically processes this input and tries to align head and belly button accordingly. Flexibility training complements resistance training and enhances skill training. Training should also be cross-specific wherever possible, sequenced in this order: (1) find the appropriate body position (in our case, one that mirrors a body position assumed during the pitching motion), (2) from this position, move your body through a range of motion that is as specific to the pitching motion as possible, and (3) resist (to tolerance) throughout the range of motion. In other words, proper flexibility training protocol should be (1) position specific, (2) movement specific, and (3) resistance specific.

Flexibility Exercise Positions and Motions

The three basic flexibility exercise positions are

- standing,
- against a wall, and
- on the floor.

In each of these positions, legs and arms will be held straight, supinate, and pronate. Joints will move in straight lines, in circles, and in figure eights. Joints will also work these movements while bent at various angles from 30 degrees to 180 degrees. Flexibility training should be done only to tolerance, with head, center of gravity, and balls of feet in alignment. The lower back should always be supported, and, again, each exercise should be position specific, movement specific, and finally resistance specific (where possible).

Please note that when there is no movement possible in a specific position, integrated flexibility training requires a concentric/eccentric, push/pull from the muscles involved in that position. This push/pull is neither static nor ballistic. It is simply a musculoskeletal wake-up call. Push/pull means just what it says; in every position and every angle push for three to five seconds and pull for three to five seconds, to tolerance, as many times as necessary to accomplish this loosening-up of the muscles, tendons, and ligaments involved in that position or angle.

Here is an example of using push/pull in a flexing exercise: In a floor-seated toe touch, reach toes with fingertips, stabilize that position, and without changing that position, pull back with fingers while resisting with toes for three to five seconds; then push away with toes while resisting with fingers for three to five seconds. (If you can't reach your toes to start the exercise, use a towel and do the same push/pull with the towel around the toes.)

Remember, a pitcher must be balanced, flexible in muscles and connective tissue, and stable with structure from feet to fingertips so that skill and talent can complement each other in competition. These flexibility exercises become foundation work in preparing to resistance train, skill train, and, ultimately, compete successfully with minimal risk of injury. Current research indicates that some form of low-impact "aerobic flush" (aerobic exercise) should precede any form of training—in rehab or prehab. I recommend Healthrider because it provides a total body musculoskeletal wake-up call as well as low-impact aerobics.

Flexibility Exercises in Standing Position

The first portion of your integrated flexibility training workout will be performed in a standing position. In this position you assume three stances—narrow, medium, and wide. In each of these stances you will perform a series of flexibility movements.

Narrow Stance

Position A: As shown in figure 2.1 on page 22, you assume the narrow stance by balancing on the balls of your feet. Your knees are slightly flexed. Your hands are on your knees (at least for the start of this sequence). Your head remains slightly in front of and over your belly button (your center of gravity).

Flexibility Sequence:

Flex your joints in the order they are listed below. In order to flex properly, you want to move your joints through a range of motion. Perform these motions for each joint:

- Move linearly (that is, straight right and left) for three to five reps.
- Roll the joint in a circular motion (both left and right) for three to five reps.
- Roll the joint in a figure-eight motion (both left and right) for three to five reps.

Figure 2.1   The narrow stance.

Work from the ground up following this progression:

1. Ankle joints.
2. Knee joints. (This is the only lower-body joint in this sequence to be worked at multiple angles, from a slight flex up to 90 degrees, but *never* more than 90 degrees.)
3. Hips.
4. Shoulders.
5. Elbows.

Position B: Keep the narrow stance, with a slight flex in your knees (see figure 2.2; flexed knees are like a car's shock absorbers—*never* lock them). For this sequence you will have your elbows in the Flex-T position, but your hands will be cupped together with your fingers locking. Throughout this sequence your hands will be pulling against each other, providing isometric resistance.

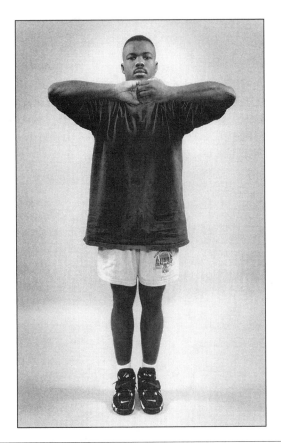

Figure 2.2   The narrow stance with elbows in the Flex-T; hands are cupped together.

Flexibility Sequence:

This exercise will improve flexibility in your shoulders. You will perform four movements from each of two forearm positions: forearms shoulder height and forearms head height.

- Move your shoulders linearly (alternating left and right shoulders) for three to five reps.
- Roll your shoulders in a circular motion (forward and backward) for three to five reps.
- Roll your shoulders in a figure-eight motion for three to five reps.
- Press-downs, press-ups, with elbows, forearms, and hands for three to five reps.

Medium Stance

Position A: As figure 2.3 shows, stand with feet approximately 12 inches apart. Keep your balance on the balls of your feet with your knees flexed. Place your hands on your knees (at least for the start of this flexibility sequence) and make sure your head remains slightly in front of and over your belly button (your center of gravity).

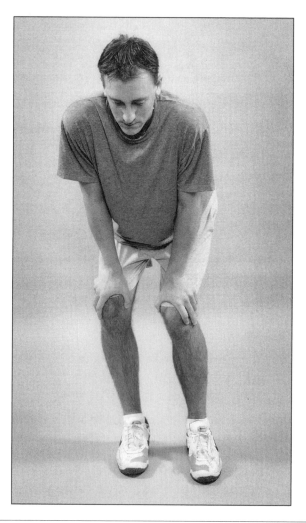

Figure 2.3   The medium stance.

Flexibility Sequence:

With your hands pushing on the sides of your knees

- move your knees linearly left and right for three to five reps,
- roll your knees in a circular motion (both left and right) for three to five reps (as shown in Figure 2.3), and
- roll your knees in a figure-eight motion for three to five reps.

Position B: Take the position shown in figure 2.4. Your knees are bent and your hands are on the floor.

Flexibility Sequence:

This is a sequence of reverse toe touches. You assume the finish position (with your hands on the floor and your knees bent), and you unbend your knees (to tolerance) without lifting your hands from the floor.

Figure 2.4   Reverse toe touch position with the toes forward.

- Perform three to five reverse toe touches with your toes pointing forward.
- Next, point your toes in like a pigeon and perform three to five reverse toe touches.
- Next, point your toes out like a duck and perform three to five reverse toe touches.

Position C: Take the position shown in figure 2.5. Your hands are comfortably clasped in front of your shoulders in a Flex-T to help with balance as you squat at the three positions.

Figure 2.5   Squat ready position with elbows in Flex-T.

Flexibility Sequence:

Keeping feet flat, squat down to tolerance with your head forward and over your belly button. This also helps you achieve dynamic balance.

- Three to five squats with your toes pointing forward.
- Next, point your toes in like a pigeon and perform three to five squats.
- Next, point your toes out like a duck and perform three to five squats.

Wide Stance

Position A: As figure 2.6 shows, stand with feet approximately four feet apart. Position the insides of your legs for the shape of what the Japanese call the *power pyramid*. Keep your balance on the balls of your feet. Your knees are flexed. Your hands are on your knees (at least for the start of this flexibility sequence). Your head remains in front of and over your belly button (your center of gravity).

Figure 2.6   The power pyramid.

Flexibility Sequence:

Place your hands on the outsides of your knees; use them to provide resistance to your knees throughout this flex.

- Move your knees linearly left and right for three to five reps.
- Roll your knee joints in a circular fashion for three to five reps.
- Roll your knee joints in a figure-eight fashion for three to five reps.

Position B: Take the position shown in figure 2.7. Your knees are bent and your hands are flat on the floor. Your legs are still forming the power pyramid.

Figure 2.7   The power pyramid with hands on floor.

Flexibility Sequence:

1. From this position perform three to five repetitions of "back push-ups" by straightening your knees and then bending them again.
2. Next perform three to five repetitions of bottom circles. Assume the starting position for a back push-up, but move your bottom in a circular motion.
   - Bottom circles to the right
   - Bottom circles to the left

3. Next perform three repetitions of left and right hamstring flexes. With your hands still on the ground lean left and then lean right keeping toes straight (see figure 2.8).
4. Now perform three repetitions of left and right hamstring stretches. This time when you lean left, you will point your right foot out. When you lean right, you will point your left foot out (see figure 2.9).

Figures 2.8 and 2.9   Leaning left and right from the power pyramid with your hands on the floor to perform (2.8) hamstring flexes and (2.9) hamstring stretches.

Position C: Stand with your feet together, knees slightly flexed, and your hands on your hips. Your head should be forward and over your belly button. This will be the starting position for a sequence of lunges and slides.

Flexibility Sequence:

1. Perform a series of three to five forward lunges alternately placing the left foot and the right foot forward. When lunging, lean, lift your lead foot off the floor, and cock your knee toward your belly button to absorb energy. Direct the energy forward as you lunge forward—keep your head over your center of gravity and your posture stable. Deliver the foot forward: strike the ball of the landing foot to the floor. During the whole motion you should think "absorb, direct, and deliver the energy" (see figure 2.10).

Figure 2.10 The "absorb," "direct," and "deliver" phases of the forward lunge.

"deliver"

Figure 2.10 *continued*

2. Perform a series of three to five backward lunges alternating the right and left feet going backward. As with the forward lunges, absorb, direct, and deliver the energy.

3. Next perform a series of three to five strides to the right, alternating with three to five strides to the left. On a side stride, cock your knee toward your belly button to absorb energy and stride to the right. At footstrike, you glide so that your torso and body weight continues linearly toward your direction of movement. When your torso and body weight has transferred to your right foot, you twist your trunk toward the direction of movement. This trunk rotation should be delayed as long as possible (while still maintaining a fluid motion). The keys to remember are "stride, glide, and rotate late" (see figure 2.11 on next page).

Figure 2.11   "Stride," "glide," and "rotate late." This can also be done with dumbbells and arms in the Flex-T.

Flexibility Exercises at the Wall

The second portion of your integrated flexibility training workout will be performed while you are pressing against a wall. First you will lie down and wiggle to the wall. Then you will place your feet, knees, legs, and butt up on the wall and use it as leverage to perform more flexibility exercises.

Position A: Lie on your back 6 to 10 feet from a wall with your legs pointing toward the wall. Raise your legs. Keep your knees bent at 90 degrees (see figure 2.12).

Figure 2.12 Getting ready to inchworm to the wall.

Flexibility Sequence: Inchworm to the wall by using your legs, spine, and elbows. Curl your spine by bringing your knees to your belly button to absorb energy, extend your legs straight out toward the wall to direct energy, and use your elbows as levers to deliver energy and propel your body forward. This movement integrates abdominals and low back as you inchworm toward the wall.

Position B: At the wall, place your feet flat on the wall. Your back is on the ground. Your knees are at 90 degrees (see figure 2.13).

Figure 2.13   At the wall—your back is on the ground, your feet are on the wall, your knees are at 90 degrees.

Flexibility Sequence:

1. In position B, with your butt on the ground, move your knees and hips through the following ranges of motion:
   - First move your knees linearly, swinging your hips side to side (three to five reps).
   - Next move your knees in a circular motion, circling your hips (three to five reps).
   - Then move your knees to make a figure eight—you'll have to roll your hips (three to five reps).
2. Now from position B, with the support of your arms and elbows, lift your back off the ground so that your butt is in the air. Your feet are still flat on the wall (see figure 2.14). Move your knees and hips through the following ranges of motion:

Figure 2.14 With your arms and elbows for support, lift your butt in the air.

- First move your knees linearly, swinging your hips side to side (three to five reps).
- Next move your knees in a circular motion, circling your hips (three to five reps).
- Then move your knees to make a figure eight—you'll have to roll your hips (three to five reps).

3. While in the butt-up position, unroll your spine back down so your butt touches the ground; then roll the spine again so you retake the butt-up position. Perform a set of three to five of these butt-ups.

4. Now from the butt-down position, put your hands behind your head and lift your shoulders off the ground to perform some sets of stomach crunches.
   - Perform a set of three to five stomach crunches with your head curling up forward.
   - Perform a set of three to five stomach crunches with your head twisting right.
   - Perform a set of three to five stomach crunches with your head twisting left.

Position C: Now inchworm even closer to the wall. Straighten your legs flat against the wall and have your butt up against the wall (see figure 2.15).

Figure 2.15   Legs straight against the wall.

Flexibility Sequence:

1. In position C, with your butt on the wall, move your legs and hips through the following ranges of motion:
   - First move your hips linearly, swinging them side to side (three to five reps).
   - Next move your hips in a circular motion (three to five reps).
   - Then move your hips to make a figure eight—you'll have to roll them (three to five reps).

2. Now from position C, with the support of your arms and elbows, lift your back off the ground so that your butt is in the air. Put your feet flat on the wall and your knees at 90 to 120 degrees (see figure 2.16).

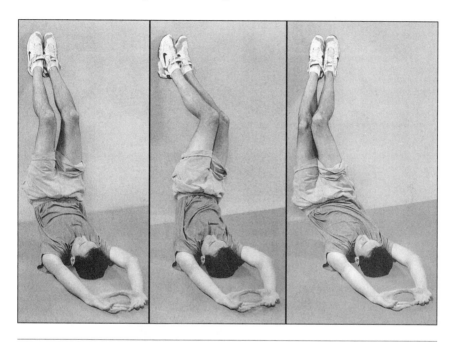

Figure 2.16 With your knees now bent at an angle, move your knees linearly, swinging your hips side to side.

Move your knees and hips through the following ranges of motion:
- First move your knees linearly, swinging your hips side to side (three to five reps) (see figure 2.16).
- Next move your knees in a circular motion, circling your hips (three to five reps).
- Then move your knees to make a figure eight—you'll have to roll your hips (three to five reps).

3. While in this butt-up position, unroll your spine back down so your butt touches the wall, then roll the spine again so you retake the butt-up position. Perform a set of three to five of these butt-ups (see figure 2.17, page 38).

Figure 2.17   Butt-ups with legs high on the wall.

4. Now from the butt-on-the-wall position, put your hands behind straight over your head and lift your shoulders off the ground to perform some sets of stomach crunches.
   - Perform a set of three to five stomach crunches with your head curling up forward and your hands reaching up to about your knees.
   - Perform a set of three to five stomach crunches with your head twisting right and your hands reaching to the right of your knees.
   - Perform a set of three to five stomach crunches with your head twisting left and your hands reaching to the left of your knees.

Position D: Now put your butt and feet on the wall, with your knees flexed at a 90- to 120-degree angle (see figure 2.18).

Figure 2.18   Put your butt and feet on the wall. Keep your knees flexed at 90 to 120 degrees.

Flexibility Sequence:

1. In position D, with your butt on the wall, move your knees and hips through the following ranges of motion:
   - First move your knees linearly, swinging your hips side to side (three to five reps).
   - Next move your knees in a circular motion, circling your hips (three to five reps).
   - Then move your knees to make a figure eight—you'll have to roll your hips (three to five reps).
2. Now from position D, with the support of your arms and elbows, lift your back off the ground so that your butt is in the air. Your feet are still on the wall and your knees are at 90 to 120 degrees.

Move your knees and hips through the following ranges of motion:

- First move your knees linearly, swinging your hips side to side (three to five reps).
- Next move your knees in a circular motion, circling your hips (three to five reps).
- Then move your knees to make a figure eight—you'll have to roll your hips (three to five reps).

3. While in this butt-up position, unroll your spine back down so your butt touches the wall, then roll the spine again so you retake the butt-up position. Perform a set of three to five of these butt-ups.

4. Now from the butt-on-the-wall position, put your hands behind your head and lift your shoulders off the ground to perform some sets of stomach crunches.

- Perform a set of three stomach crunches with your head curling up forward.
- Perform a set of three stomach crunches with your head twisting right.
- Perform a set of three stomach crunches with your head twisting left.

Position E: Now put your butt and feet on the wall, with your knees flexed at an angle of 90 degrees or less. You want to have your heels as close to your butt as possible (see figure 2.19).

Flexibility Sequence:

1. In position E, with your butt on the wall, move your knees and hips through the following ranges of motion:

- First move your knees linearly, swinging your hips side to side (three to five reps).
- Next move your knees in a circular motion, circling your hips (three to five reps).
- Then move your knees to make a figure eight—you'll have to roll your hips (three to five reps).

2. Now from position E, with the support of your arms and elbows, lift your back off the ground so that your butt is in the air. Your feet are still on the wall and your knees are at an angle of 90 degrees or less.

Figure 2.19   Put your butt and feet on the wall. Keep your knees flexed at less than a 90-degree angle.

Move your knees through the following ranges of motion:

- First move your knees linearly, swinging your hips side to side (three to five reps).
- Next move your knees in a circular motion, circling your hips (three to five reps).
- Then move your knees to make a figure eight—you'll have to roll your hips (three to five reps).

3. While in this butt-up position, unroll your spine back down so your butt hits the wall; then roll the spine again so you retake the butt-up position (three to five reps).

4. Now from the butt-on-the-wall position, put your hands behind your head and lift your shoulders off the ground to perform some sets (three to five reps) of stomach crunches.

- Perform a set of crunches with your head curling up forward.
- Perform a set with your head twisting right.
- Perform a set with your head twisting left.

Position F: Keep your butt against the wall, but put your feet together "Indian style" so that the soles of both feet are pointing inward and touching (see figure 2.20).

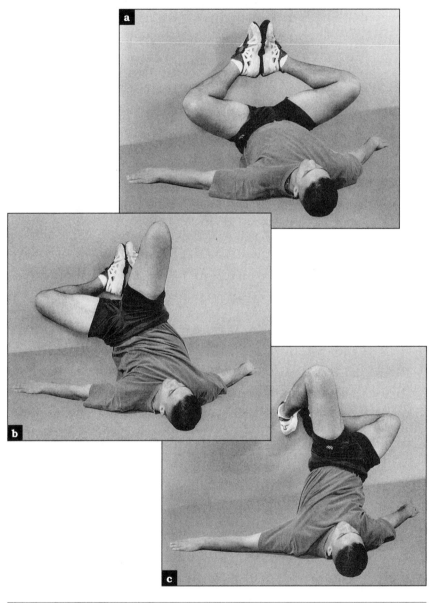

Figure 2.20 Performing figure eights from the Indian-style, butt-against-the-wall position.

Flexibility Sequence:

1. In position F, with your butt on the wall and the soles of your feet together, move your knees and hips through the following ranges of motion:

   - First move your knees linearly, swinging your hips side to side (three to five reps).
   - Next move your knees in a circular motion, circling your hips (three to five reps).
   - Then move your hips to make a figure eight—you'll have to roll them (three to five reps) (see figure 2.20a).

2. Now from position F, with the support of your arms and elbows, lift your back off the ground so that your butt is in the air. Your feet are still on the wall and your soles are still together Indian style.

   Move your knees through a range of motion by moving your hips.

   - First move your knees linearly, swinging your hips side to side (three to five reps).
   - Next move your knees in a circular motion, circling your hips (three to five reps).
   - Then move your knees to make a figure eight—you'll have to roll your hips (three to five reps). (See figures 2.20b-c.)

3. While in this butt-up position with your legs still Indian style, unroll your spine back down so your butt touches the wall; then roll the spine again so you retake the butt-up position. Perform a set of three to five of these butt-ups.

4. Now from the butt-on-the-wall position with your legs still Indian style, put your hands behind your head and lift your shoulders off the ground to perform some sets of stomach crunches.

   - Perform a set of three to five stomach crunches with your head curling up forward.
   - Perform a set of three to five stomach crunches with your head twisting right.
   - Perform a set of three to five stomach crunches with your head twisting left.

5. In the Indian-style, butt-on-the-wall position, put your hands on your knees and push outward to tolerance three to five seconds; then push your knees back into your hands to tolerance three to five seconds to flex your groin.

Flexibility Exercises on the Floor

The third and final portion of your integrated flexibility training workout will be performed while you are on the floor. First you will lie belly-up for some exercises; then you will perform some flexibility exercises in a sitting position; and finally you will finish your integrated flexibility program workout lying belly-down.

Belly-Up Flexibility Exercises on the Floor

Position A: Lie flat on the floor with your legs straight, your arms and hands above your head. Make yourself as long as you can. Try to push your arms, head, back, butt, and legs through the floor. Push through the floor for three to five seconds and release the tension. Do three to five sets of these pushes.

Flexibility Sequence:

1. From position A, put your hands on your thighs to perform your first set of "elbow-ups." There are four elbow-ups involving four different hand/forearm positions:
   - With hands *on your thighs* perform three to five elbow-ups using your elbows to lift shoulders and head off the floor. When you can do this movement comfortably "squinch" (squeeze and pinch) your shoulder blades together when shoulders and head are up.
   - With your hands *on your belly button* (see figure 2.21), perform a set of three to five elbow-ups with shoulder blade squinches.

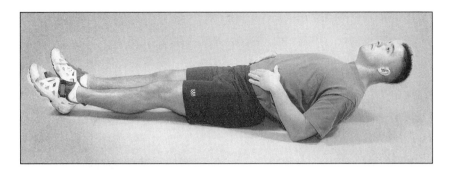

Figure 2.21   Elbow-ups with hands on belly button.

- With your thumbs in your arm pits, perform a set of three to five elbow-ups with shoulder blade squinches.
- With your hands behind your head, perform a set of three to five elbow-ups with shoulder blade squinches.
2. With your hands on your hips and using your elbows for support, lift your butt and torso about one inch off the floor, stabilizing your head, heels, and elbows on the floor to tolerance. I call this the head-and-heel body bridge (see figure 2.22).

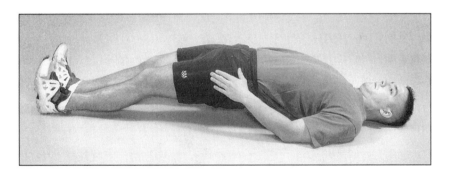

Figure 2.22   The head-and-heel body bridge.

Position B: From position A, draw up your feet so that your knees are at a 90° angle, lift your shoulders and head off the ground to perform a series of crunches. Try not to let your shoulders and head touch the ground until you complete *all* crunches in the following sequences.

Flexibility Sequence:

1. Perform a series of crunches.
   - Try to touch your knees and elbows (three to five reps).
   - Try to touch your left elbow to your right knee (three to five reps).
   - Try to touch your right elbow to your left knee (three to five reps).
2. Next, from the crunch position extend your legs forward, keeping shoulders, head, and feet off the ground, until your knees are straight.
   - Lift and extend your legs forward (three to five reps).
   - Lift and extend your legs left foot over right, making a circular motion with your hips to keep the motion a fluid roll (three to five reps) (see figure 2.23).

Figure 2.23   Crunching and extending left.

- Lift and extend your legs right foot over left, making a circular motion with your hips to keep the motion a fluid roll (three to five reps).

3. Perform a set of Indian-style crunches. Assume this crunch position by putting the soles of your feet together so that your knees flare out, shoulders and head off the ground.
   - Crunch straight ahead (three to five reps).
   - Crunch so your left elbow goes toward your right knee (three to five reps).
   - Crunch so your right elbow goes toward your left knee (three to five reps).

Sitting-Up Flexibility Exercises on the Floor

Position A: Sit up with your legs together out before you. Your palms are flat on the floor beside your hips and your upper-body posture is slightly forward with your head over and slightly in front of your belly button.

Flexibility Sequence:

1. Work your shoulder muscles by performing sets of butt-ups by lifting your butt up off the floor.
   - Perform three to five butt-ups with your arms in the linear (fastball—palms forward) position.
   - Perform three to five butt-ups with your arms in the supinate (breaking ball—palms away from your body) position.
   - Perform three to five butt-ups with your arms in the pronate (change up—palms toward your body) position.
   - Perform three to five butt-ups with your arms in a reverse linear (palms backward) position.

2. Now lean forward and grab your toes (if you can reach that far—if not, use a towel and flex only to tolerance). Pull against your toes with your fingers and push against your fingers with your toes for a count of three to five seconds. Do three to five reps.

3. Spread your legs apart so that the angle between them is 90°. Hold each position for three to five seconds and do three to five reps.

- Lean right and grab your right toes with your right hand. Pull against your toes with your fingers and push against your fingers with your toes.
- Lean left and grab your left toe with your left hand. Pull against your toes with your fingers and push against your fingers with your toes.
- Lean forward and grab your right toes with your right hand and your left toes with your left hand. Pull against your toes with your fingers and push against your fingers with your toes.

4. Draw your legs up Indian style so the soles of your feet are touching. Lean forward slightly. Rest your elbows high on the inside of your knees. Your hands and arms should point forward. Press down with your elbows while pressing up with your knees for a count of three to five seconds (three to five reps).

5. Now assume the pretzel position shown in figure 2.24. Push right with your right elbow and resist with your left knee for three to five seconds. Do three to five reps. Then

Figure 2.24   The pretzel stretch.

switch legs and arms so that you push your left elbow against your right knee for three to five seconds. Perform three to five reps.

Belly-Down Flexibility Exercises on the Floor

Position A: Assume a "Moslem prayer" position (see figure 2.25). You are on your knees and forearms with your torso leaning forward. Keep your weight evenly supported and drop your torso as low to the ground as possible.

Figure 2.25 Praying to the right and to the left .

Flexibility Sequence:

- "Pray" with your arms out in front of you (three to five seconds).

- "Pray" with your arms over to your left side (three to five seconds).
- "Pray" with your arms over to your right side (three to five seconds).

Position B: Now glide your forearms forward until your back is straight and you are lying face down. Put your arms out in front of you so you are lying as tall as you can. The object is to have as much of your body touch the floor as possible.

Flexibility Sequence:

1. Perform a set of abdominal pushes. Create the feeling that you are pushing your back through your belly button and right through the floor. Hold the tension for three to five seconds. Perform three to five sets.
2. Perform a sequence of "Supermans." To do a basic Superman, lift your arms, head, and legs up off the ground as high as possible to tolerance.
   - Perform a set of three to five basic Supermans with head up and both legs and arms lifted.
   - Perform a set of three to five Supermans lifting your right arm and left leg simultaneously (see figure 2.26).
   - Perform a set of three to five Supermans lifting your left arm and right leg simultaneously.
   - Perform a set of three to five Supermans lifting your right arm and right leg simultaneously.

Figure 2.26 A superman sequence: lifting your right arm and left leg simultaneously.

- Perform a set of three to five Supermans lifting your left arm and left leg simultaneously.
- Perform a set of three to five Supermans lifting your hands up first and then your feet.
- Perform a set of three to five Supermans lifting your feet up first and then your hands.

3. Perform a sequence of forearm-ups. Keeping your belly button and legs *flat* on the ground, bring your forearms and elbows to a position in front of your chest. Arch your back and lift your shoulders and head as high as possible, to tolerance (see figure 2.27).

Figure 2.27 Forearm-ups—performed with hands in the straight, pronate, and supinate positions.

- Perform three to five forearm-ups, squeezing shoulder blades together with your arms in the straight (fastball) position.
- Perform three to five forearm-ups, squeezing shoulder blades together with your arms in the supinate (breaking ball) position.
- Perform three to five forearm-ups, squeezing shoulder blades together with your arms in the pronate (change-up) position.

4. Perform a sequence of head and temple presses with your upper arms positioned in a Flex-T, forearms resting on the ground. From this position try to press your head down through the floor, to tolerance.

- Press your forehead for three to five seconds.
- Look to your right and press your left temple for three to five seconds.
- Look to your left and press your right temple for three to five seconds.

5. Perform a sequence of "cobras." Lift your torso up so your weight is supported by your forearms; keep your belly button and everything south of it on the floor (see figure 2.28). Think of yourself as a cobra about to strike.

- Take the cobra position and look straight.
- Take the cobra position and twist your head and torso to look right.
- Take the cobra position and twist your head and torso to look left.

Position C: Assume a balanced position on hands and knees to perform a series of "cats" (see figure 2.29).

- Perform a mad cat by arching your back upward.
- Perform a fat cat by pushing your stomach and lower back toward floor.
- Perform a cat right by twisting your head and torso to look right.
- Perform a cat left by twisting your head and torso to look left.

Figure 2.28   Cobra right and cobra left.

Figure 2.29   Cat right.

Position D: Assume the basic Flex-T push-up position for a series of push-ups.

- Perform three to five push-ups with your arms in a straight (fastball) position.
- Perform three to five push-ups with your arms in a supinate (breaking ball) position.
- Perform three to five push-ups with your arms in a pronate (change-up) position.

Flexibility Training Summary

An athlete's body is subject to all the laws of physics, including action/reaction and inertia. Players' muscles and connective tissue are also subject to the law of use and disuse. In other words, use it or lose it! Integrated flexibility training lays a foundation for talent and skill to perform in competition by using every body part, in every linear and angular position, through every movement, in every range of motion, every day. The exercise protocol presented in this chapter should become part of the way you prepare yourself to pitch. It's a perfect lead-in to the next phase of being fit to pitch: aerobic and anaerobic conditioning.

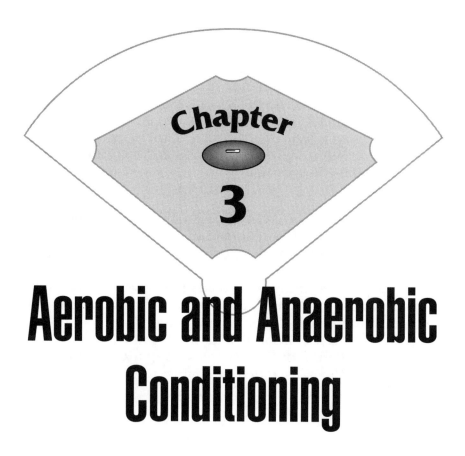

Aerobic and Anaerobic Conditioning

> **The only time I worry about air is when there isn't any—like every day about my fourth sprint!**
>
> **Charlie Kerfeld, former Houston Astros pitcher**

At six feet six inches and 270 something pounds, Charlie wasn't fond of either aerobic or anaerobic work. Most ballplayers, in fact, consider aerobic and anaerobic training the worst part of their conditioning: unnecessary drudgery is how they view it. Given the choice, players would much rather work their muscles in the weight room. Muscle strength and muscle endurance training, however, are only one leg of physical conditioning. Aerobic and anaerobic training, or stamina, is the other leg, and both legs must be properly prepared. To clear up misinformation about the cardiovascular and respiratory side of a pitcher's fitness program, I've included a question-and-answer section about aerobics, anaerobics, and how they apply to a pitcher's stamina.

What is aerobic work and what is its purpose?

Aerobic work puts oxygen in the body. When heart and lungs get more oxygenated blood to the body, the contractive properties of working muscle tissue are facilitated, more lactic acid (the stuff that makes your muscles fatigue and ache) is neutralized, and wounds are healed more quickly. Ultimately, the body trains more efficiently before competition and the arm recovers more rapidly after competition. There is another major benefit derived from regular aerobic work: it burns fat. This is a real bonus because nerves do not work in fat and because four times as much energy is required to move a pound of fat than a pound of lean muscle.

What is anaerobic work and what is its purpose?

Anaerobic work puts the body in oxygen debt. Done regularly, this increases lung capacity (as measured by $\dot{V}O_2max$). Increased lung capacity means more oxygen is available with each breath to push back the wall of fatigue and muscle failure.

What is considered proper aerobic/anaerobic work for a pitcher?

Proper aerobic/anaerobic work is finding the right combination of both variables so that they match up with a pitcher's strength training, his skill training, and his competitive role (starter or reliever) in both his micro and macro cycles.

Aerobic and anaerobic work builds an efficient stamina base that enhances (1) preparation for performance, (2) performance, and (3) recovery from performance—three necessary and achievable goals for any competitive athlete, but especially for a pitcher. Now if you're following me, other questions naturally arise:

- What is the proper way to build an efficient stamina base?
- Is there a set program that works best for a starter?
- Is the program different for a reliever?
- If different, what mix works best for starters?
- What mix works best for relievers?

Let's approach individual components, identify a starter/ reliever mix, and answer a few more aerobic and anaerobic questions.

Aerobic Conditioning

Aerobic work, as we've discussed, means putting oxygen into the body. Don't work too intensely. During any aerobic conditioning activity, work to the level of effort at which you can carry on a conversation without gasping for breath. Train 25 to 45 minutes, three to seven times per week. That's a wide range of duration and frequency guidelines, I know. But the proper duration and frequency of aerobic conditioning are a function of when and how skill training, resistance work, and nutrition (blood chemistry) training protocols are integrated during in-season and off-season. An athlete's metabolism will stabilize to the level of aerobic fitness necessary for the demands placed on his body. Generally, however, you'll train periodically with the same duration and frequency as your competitive job description, both in-season *and* off-season, around resistance-training constraints. The only exception would be for weight control and fat burning. Losing excess body fat might require 30 to 45 minutes of aerobic activity every day on top of all your other training!

What choices does a pitcher have for aerobic work? It is a big menu; all these activities train aerobic fitness:

- Brisk walking, with or without hand weights, to tolerance.
- Jogging at an easy nine-minute-per-mile pace to tolerance.
- Biking (regular or stationary) to tolerance.

- Machine work to tolerance.
  - —Healthrider* (see figure 3.1)
  - —Treadmill
  - —Stairmaster
  - —Versa Climber
  - —NordicTrack
  - —Rowing machine
- Pool work to tolerance.
  - —Swimming
  - —Treading water
  - —Shallow-end running
  - —Kicking, paddling

Figure 3.1   The Healthrider is an aerobic and a closed chain conditioning machine. Notice also that you can combine specificity training principles—here I have my arms in the pronated position.

*Healthrider can also double as a "closed chain" conditioning machine for strength building lean muscle mass. This will be discussed further in chapters 5 and 9 as body work.

The key is not in the method, it is in the mode. To be effective, aerobic work must be a consistent, predictable, and sustained effort. Ask your heart to beat faster and your lungs to breathe deeper for an extended time to give your total body a regular aerobic flush. I tell pitchers that aerobics changes their oil.

Anaerobic Conditioning

If aerobic work changes the body's oil, anaerobic work helps insure that the blood chemistry has a high-octane oxygen content. Challenging lung capacity with oxygen debt increases lung capacity. Alveoli, the lung tissue that pulls O_2 out of the air, get more efficient in this expanded capacity, transporting more oxygen into the blood and ultimately to tissues requiring oxygen for training and competition. The wall of oxygen debt gets pushed back during physical activity and, just as important, recovery cycles are shortened proportionately. So, increasing lung capacity ($\dot{V}O_2$max) delivers more oxygen to the circulatory system, more oxygen to working muscle tissue, and more oxygen to tissue recovering from muscle failure. It's high octane for high performance!

What are the choices for a pitcher's anaerobic work? Here, too, there are many choices, all of which can reduce a pitcher to oxygen debt and build $\dot{V}O_2$max very effectively:

1. Interval training is a form of sprint work set up to keep heart rate and breathing rate accelerated to a maximal plateau. Coach and pitcher predetermine a heart rate and breathing rate for sprints of specified distance and time, for both macro and micro training cycles. Thus, spring-training (macro) intervals will be different than in-season, between-start (micro) intervals, both in duration and intensity.

2. Plyometrics are explosive movements involving the total body in jumping, lunging, striding, sprinting, and thrusting. In-season plyos should be low impact only—skipping, long/short strides, butt kickers, kariokas, running backward, and/or pool work. Save the high-impact plyometric work for off-season. Jumping and lunging with one or two legs, up and

down boxes or steps, over cords, or with and against elastic resistance are all great for an athlete's $\dot{V}O_2$max and fast-twitch explosiveness, but not when he is competing three to seven times per week.

3. Jumping rope is a high-impact cross-trainer combining plyometric and interval applications.

4. Pool work is a low-impact cross-trainer combining plyometric and interval applications.

All anaerobic training methods should be cross-specific to the physical movement required of a pitcher's delivery and defense, at a level of intensity that challenges an athlete toward peak performance. But the method must account for prehab and rehab cycles. Push to maximum tolerance, but *not* to breakdown.

Let's get a little more specific with the four anaerobic conditioning protocols.

Run/Walk Intervals

Performance: Off-season or spring training only, starters and relievers together.

Start at LF foul line, stay on field perimeters in clockwise rotations (see figure 3.2):

a) Run to CF, walk briskly to RF foul line.
b) Run RF foul line to LF foul line (in front of both dugouts behind home plate), walk briskly to CF.
c) Run CF to LF foul line, walk briskly to CF.
d) Run CF to CF, walk briskly to RF foul line.
e) Run RF foul line to CF, walk briskly to RF foul line.
f) Run RF foul line to LF foul line, walk briskly to CF.
g) Run CF to RF foul line, walk briskly from foul line to LF foul line (cool-down).

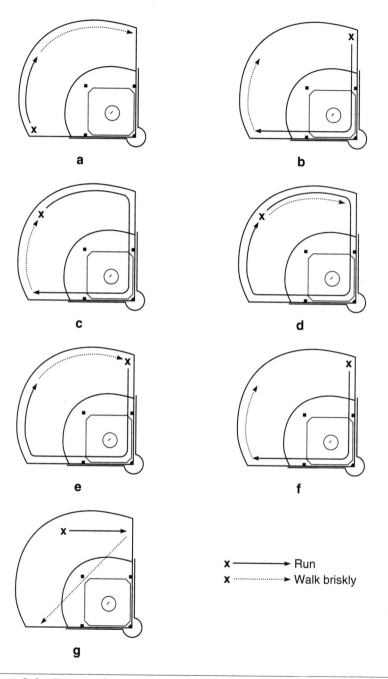

Figure 3.2   Run/walk intervals.

Relay Plyos

Performance: In-season, starters and relievers together.

Divide pitchers into three groups (as shown in figure 3.3). Groups 1 and 3 stay on LF line; group 2 jogs out toward CF, at "X" distance. Make sure a starter is in each group:

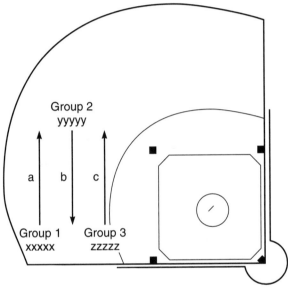

Figure 3.3   Relay plyos.

   a) Group 1 runs to group 2 in CF.
   b) Group 2 runs to group 3 on LF foul line.
   c) Group 3 runs to group 1 in CF.

In these rotations the pitchers will do the following plyos (starting pitchers should always do more than relievers, especially yesterday's starter):

- Three to five sprints (with short strides)
- Three to five kariokas
- Three to five skips

- Three to five runs backward
- Three to five sprints (with long strides)

You can vary the number of plyos and distances. Other anaerobic training methods can be mixed in with intervals and relay plyos. Remember the body gets bored with "same old same old" protocols.

Jumping Rope

Performance: Off-season with maximum intensity, to tolerance in-season, both starters and relievers.

Jumping with heavy or light rope is an indoor and outdoor $\dot{V}O_2$max cross-trainer. It can be done in submaximal intervals (in-season) or in a prolonged burst of intense maximal effort (off-season), which can reduce even the fittest of pitchers to "anaerobic protoplasm." Use rope work to overcome neural stagnation (the negative side effect of monotonous overtraining) but not in rehab situations. Like high-impact plyos, the rope is a prehab protocol designed to peak the "fit into fitter" plateaus.

Pool Work

Performance: Off-season with maximal intensity, in-season to tolerance, both starters and relievers.

Pool work is a great variation for prehab and for athletes in physical rehab. Water supports muscle, connective tissue, and bone during intervals and/or burnout bursts, thereby reducing the bone and joint pounding of running, jumping, and sliding on ground or floor. Nolan Ryan, for example, did most of his sprint work in the pool, a concession to his age and recovery cycles. Develop a program that has a pitcher doing the same anaerobic work in the water that he would do on flat ground (i.e., sprints, lunges, slides, etc.).

Training Summary

Cardiovascular and respiratory stamina is important to physical conditioning, both to prepare and repair pitchers for competition. This chapter has provided some insight and information on how better to train for aerobic and anaerobic efficiency. Nolan Ryan had one of the best analogies I have ever heard for a pitcher's in-season and game-to-game relationship: "A baseball season is like a marathon. Each game is like a single mile that the pitcher must run, but the race isn't over until he's completed all 26 miles. You've got to prepare for both the long and short of it."

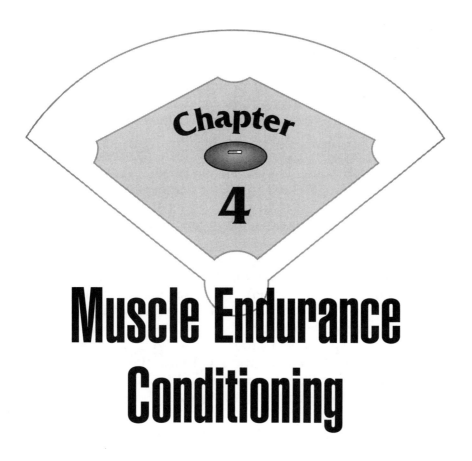

Muscle Endurance Conditioning

Your body, like a chain, is only as strong as its weakest link.

Alan Bliztblau, Bio-Kinetics Research Analyst

I have learned over the last 10 years that Alan Blitzblau's comments about human performance are just as astute as his research on human movement. When we were baselining our "weak link" hypothesis at Bio-Kinetics in 1991 and 1992, Rob

Dibble was creating a stir in Cincinnati with his mound antics and 100-mile-per-hour fastball. In analyzing his delivery, we quantified Rob's mechanics in the low to marginal range and considered him a candidate for injury. But Alan also said that there would be a strength issue—an imbalance between Dibble's absolute strength and his functional strength. It was only an observation at the time. But, as usual, Alan was prophetic. Rob's physical problems over the past few years have nothing to do with how strong he is—I'll bet he can lift more than most pitchers in either league. His problem has been that the little stuff in his shoulder has not been strong enough to handle the explosive power and energy of his big stuff.

In 30-plus years of professional baseball, I have never hurt a prime mover (a large muscle or muscle group) while throwing a baseball, nor have I seen any other pitcher hurt a large muscle group by just throwing. Pitchers' injuries invariably occur in connective tissue and small muscle groups. To that end, whenever possible, prime movers should be trained *after* training connective tissue and small muscle groups. Muscle balance and muscle endurance should be addressed *before* muscle strength, and *functional* strength should have priority over *absolute* strength.

This is a departure from the norm. Traditionally, resistance training has been prime-mover oriented with a focus on absolute strength. It hasn't worked for baseball. What does work is a program that incorporates the following overall objectives:

• Resistance training that integrates muscles, tendons, ligaments, and bone through positions and movements specific to the positions and movements involved in the skill of *throwing a baseball.*

• Sequencing this training with protocols that are position specific, then movement specific, and finally resistance specific to the skills involved in *playing baseball.*

• Balancing all resistance work right to left, concentric to eccentric, front-side muscle tissues (the accelerators when you pitch) and back-side muscle tissues (the decelerators when you pitch). It's also best to work the back side at one-third more in volume, or repetitions, than the front side. This overcomes a basic imbalance which preexists in all pitchers when they throw off a mound: Three muscle groups accelerate the arm in x amount of time, while two muscle groups have to decelerate the arm in one-half x time.

The goal of muscle strength/muscle endurance conditioning is a body that has enough balanced strength to handle the demands of mechanical efficiency for the number of pitches an athlete throws in a given week. Specifically, we are looking for trunk stabilization and scapular stabilization as the body directs energy in weight transfer and translates energy from feet to fingertips into the release of the baseball. Remember, the training sequence for pitchers is critical: integrated flexibility first, then connective tissue and small muscle groups, and finally large muscle groups. Also, pitchers must loosen up to warm up to do resistance activities. Before touching a weight of any variety, a pitcher should do 15 to 45 minutes of aerobic work to get the blood circulating and heat up the body from within (this is especially important in rehab). Once this is accomplished, athletes can do elastic cord work, light dumbbell work, medicine ball work, and pool work for their connective tissue and small muscle group training. Since none of these exercises puts a pitcher in muscle failure, any one, or any combination, of these exercises can be done every day, inseason or off-season.

Elastic Cord Work

Elastic cord work should precede light dumbbell work. The elastic cord is a complement to the dumbbells because it can be isometric, as well as isotonic, work. Plus, depending on how far the cord is stretched, resistance can be increased or decreased as a function of how the athlete feels in his workout (i.e., tolerance).

The elastic cord is a cross-specific mechanics-training and resistance-training device for both prehabilitation and rehabilitation. It can be used on and off the field, in any phase of preparation, for skill work or competition (i.e., as low resistance/low intensity activities for loosening-up, as medium resistance/medium intensity activities for warming-up, or as high resistance/high intensity activities for strength training). The key to the integrated protocol is in the sequencing and/or positioning of torso and limbs specific to the movements of the pitching mechanics you are training on the field (i.e., position specific, resistance specific, movement specific *to tolerance*, for whatever phase of preparation or recovery the player is in).

Elastic cord work yields maximum return with minimum risk and you are training skill while training strength. Elastic resistance training is an important part of a pitcher's workout continuum, both in-season and off-season. Anchor your elastic cord to a post or weight machine for these four exercises:

1. High-elbow swims: forward and reverse (see figure 4.1), 5 to 15 reps.
2. High-elbow hitchhikes: right arm, left arm (see figure 4.2), 5 to 15 reps.
3. Thumbs-ups and thumbs-downs: both arms (see figure 4.3), 5 to 15 reps.

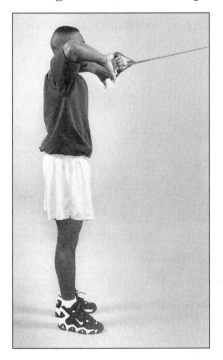 

Figure 4.1   High-elbow swims forward.

Figure 4.2 Hitchhikes.

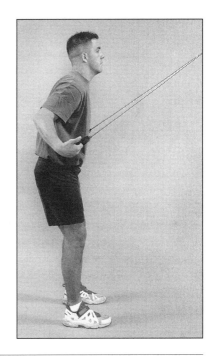

Figure 4.3 Thumbs-up.

4. Why me's: thumbs down and thumbs up (see figure 4.4),
   5 to 15 reps.

Figure 4.4   A why me?

Light Dumbbell Work

Light dumbbells—I call them training wheels—are 3- to 10-pound weights lifted in 12 sets at three angles of 3 to 5 reps and/or three rotations of 3 to 5 reps with intensity. Intensity means backing up sets, one right after another, allowing little or no rest between the movement sets. Within each dumbbell exercise, linear and rotational movements simulate fastball, breaking ball, and change-up forearm positions through a cross-specific range of motion with shoulders and elbows in each set.

The light dumbbells recruit blood flow to connective tissue and small muscle groups *before* big muscle prime movers take over—sort of a reverse pyramiding effect. As with the elastic cord, the sequencing and/or positioning of torso and limbs must always be cross-specific to the mechanics of pitching.

The following pages illustrate 11 light dumbbell exercises.

1. Start with weights, elbows, and shoulders in a Flex-T position. Alternate extending your arms to full reach. Then alternate straight up; then rotate your palms out (change-up) or in (breaking ball) during extension. Do 5 to 15 total reps.

2. Start with weights at sides. Bring your right arm to left shoulder, bending elbow with palm up going up, palm down going down. Repeat with left arm touching right shoulder (see figure 4.5). Do a set of 5 to 15 reps. Repeat the sequence with palm down going up and palm up going down.

Figure 4.5 Bring your right arm up to your left shoulder and your left arm up to your right shoulder.

3. Start with weights hanging behind your head, and your elbows and shoulders held as high as possible in a narrow Flex-T. Alternate extending to full reach. When arms are extended, they should be slightly in front of or behind your head, not directly above (see figure 4.6). Do a set of 5 to 15 reps. Then repeat the sequence twice: once with the arms coming up while the wrists rotate palm in (breaking ball) and once with the arms coming up while the wrists rotate palm out (change-up).

Figure 4.6 Start with weights behind your head and extend to full reach.

4. Start with weights hanging at your sides. Alternating arms, lift across your body at a 45-degree angle to shoulder height (see figure 4.7). Pretend your shoulders are against a wall and keep them there with each lift. Do a set of 5 to 15 reps. Then repeat the sequence three times: first rotating your wrists so your thumbs are up during the lift; then rotating your wrists so your thumbs are down during the lift; then rotating your wrists to the sky, with your palms facing the floor.

Figure 4.7 Lift across your body. Rotate your wrists so thumbs are up for a set. Then rotate wrists so thumbs are down for a set. Finally, rotate wrists to the sky for a set (not shown).

5. Start with weights hanging in front of groin and lift straight out and up to full extension of arms overhead. Flex your shoulders and lower back when the weights are fully extended (see figure 4.8). Do 5 to 15 reps. Then repeat the sequence three times: once with your thumbs up, once with your thumbs down, and once with your palms down. Maintain form both with the lift and when returning your hands to the starting position.

Figure 4.8   Lift straight up and out to full extension.

6. Start with weights hanging at the groin area. Lift to chest and then extend forearms into a Flex-T position with your arms fully extended (see figure 4.9). Always have weights slightly forward of the shoulders and point the thumbs down, thumbs straight, and thumbs up with the lift. Do 5 to 15 reps.

Figure 4.9   From the start position, lift to chest (as shown). Then, extend forearms into a Flex-T position with arms fully extended.

7. Start with weights touching together in front of your groin. Lift away from your body in a windmill action, touching weights at a point in front of your head (not over the top) with arms fully extended, and return slowly. Rotate your palms down and out; then rotate thumbs down, thumbs straight, and thumbs up as weights touch on top (see figure 4.10). Do the same going down. (Remember to keep your arms slightly in front of your head.) Do 5 to 15 reps.

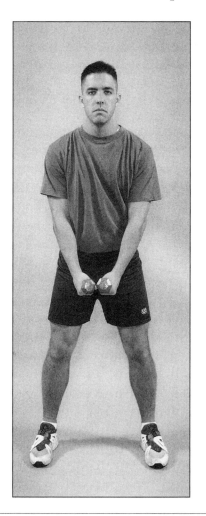 

Figure 4.10   Lift away from your body in a windmill action.

8. Bend over in a toe-touch position and let the weights rest on the floor. Alternate lifting weight to shoulder while leaving the opposite weight on the floor (see figure 4.11). Do 5 to 15 reps. Then repeat the sequence twice: first rotating the thumb forward (to tolerance) during the lift; then rotating the thumb backward (to tolerance) during the lift.

Figure 4.11 Alternate lifting weights to shoulder height.

9. Bend over into an L position. Bring elbows to shoulder height first; then extend arms straight out until parallel with the ground (see figure 4.12). Keep arms extended and return to the original position. Do 5 to 15 reps; then repeat the exercise rotating your thumbs up and your thumbs down during the extension.

Figure 4.12   Bring elbows to shoulder height first, then extend arms straight out.

10. Start with weights hanging at your sides with your palms facing back. Lift your arms (together or one at a time) until your elbow and forearm are at a 90-degree angle; then extend the weight out and up to a Flex-T, then drop forearms to shoulder height (see figure 4.13). Reverse the action to get back to the starting position. Do 5 to 15 reps. Then repeat the sequence, lifting the thumbs up in a hitchhike movement with the lift, then thumbs down.

Figure 4.13   Lift arms until elbow and forearm are at a 90-degree angle, then extend weight out and up to shoulder height.

11. Start with weights in a hands-up position with elbows and shoulders in a Flex-T. Keeping your elbows parallel to the ground, roll the weights forward to shoulder height, pause, and then roll the weights back to shoulder height, or as far as possible (see figure 4.14). Do 5 to 15 reps. Repeat the movement thumbs up, then thumbs down.

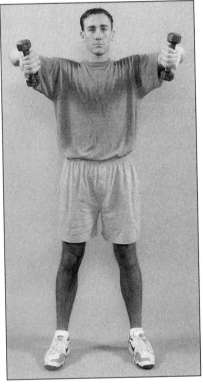

Figure 4.14 Start with weights in a hands-up position. The elbows and shoulders are in a Flex-T. Roll weights forward to shoulder height, pause, and roll back.

12. Start with throwing arm dumbbell in an elbow-shoulder-high, hitchhike-up position and the opposite arm dumbbell in an across-the-body, thumb-down, and at-hip position. Take your throwing arm to hip level and the opposite arm to the hitchhike position, making an X pattern with your arms across your torso (see figure 4.15). Rotate thumbs up to thumbs down during the movement. Do 5 to 15 reps.

Figure 4.15   In a fluid motion make an X-pattern across your torso by raising and lowering your arms.

Medicine Ball Work

The medicine ball is great for postural stabilization, scapular stabilization, and high-elbow Flex-T reinforcement, as well as for connective tissue and small muscle endurance building. The key is finding the right weight of ball and working to tolerance with *perfect* posturing in pitching-specific ranges of motion with each exercise. Try these:

1. Flex-T wall toss right, 45 to 60 reps (see figure 4.16).
2. Flex-T wall toss left, 45 to 60 reps.
3. Narrow-elbow wall bounce (figure 4.17), 45 to 60 reps.
4. Wide-elbow wall bounce (figure 4.18), 45 to 60 reps.

Figure 4.16   Flex-T wall toss right.

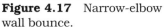

Figure 4.17   Narrow-elbow wall bounce.

Figure 4.18   Wide-elbow wall bounce.

Pool Work

Pool work allows you to train by creating your own movements. Stand chest deep in the water. Assume your pitching posture and move your arms in every angle and every range of motion possible. You can cup your hands or use paddles to vary resistance. This is great therapy for the little hot spots all pitchers get during the season. Here are four basic exercises to go with your own movements:

1. Bent-elbow palm-downs and palm-ups, 45 to 60 reps. Keeping your elbows at your sides, move your hands up to shoulder height with your palms up (to make for the greatest possible resistance), and then flip your palms over and push your hands down so they are back by your hips.
2. Bent-elbow palm-ins and palm-outs, 45 to 60 reps. With your elbows remaining close to your sides let the backs of your hands touch. Then push your hands out away from each other. To complete the exercise, flip your hands so that your palms face each other; then bring your hands together as though you're squeezing an accordion.
3. Straight-arm palm-downs and palm-ups, 45 to 60 reps. Use the same motion as the bent-elbow palm-ups and downs, except this time work the range of motion from your shoulders rather than from your elbows.
4. Straight-arm palm-ins and palm-outs, 45 to 60 reps. Use the same motion as the bent-elbow palm-ins and outs, except this time work the range of motion from your shoulders rather than from your elbows.

Training Summary

These exercises have trained your small muscles and connective tissue for endurance by sequentially loading and unloading resistance, specific to the physical act of throwing a baseball. As a pitcher, you can be confident there's enough muscle endurance and connective tissue balance in the little stuff to begin conditioning the big stuff—your large muscle groups or prime movers.

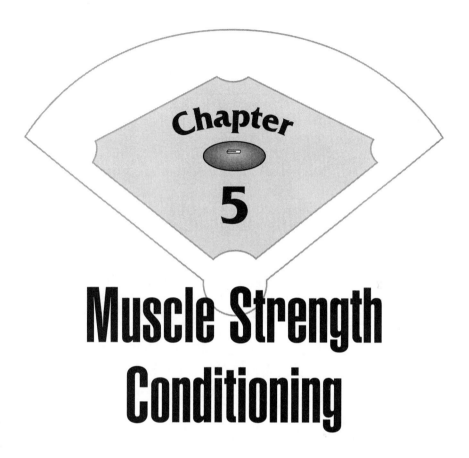

Muscle Strength Conditioning

Bulk is for the beach, density for the diamond.

Coop DeRenne, PhD (hitting coach, exercise physiologist at University of Hawaii)

By this point in the book I've discussed how to loosen up, warm up, and integrate connective tissue and small muscle strength conditioning into your training protocols. Now it's time to train the big stuff, balancing the absolute strength of your prime movers with aerobic/anaerobic stamina and muscle endurance. I'll show you how to work the prime movers in three modes: body work (in which our bodies, sometimes aided by light- to medium-weight dumbbells, provide resistance), machine work (in which the machine provides resistance, to tolerance, in a controlled range of motion), and heavy weight work (in which free weights provide resistance, to tolerance, in positions and movements specific to pitching a baseball). The following pages expand on each of these components.

Body Work

Body work, or closed chain work, is next in the resistance-training progression. If at all possible, train to a resistance volume that will match weekly throwing volumes.* Body work doesn't require a million-dollar weight room and it helps overcome the neural stagnation of monotonous overtraining that comes with traditional lifting. Also, lifting the body itself is a method to strength train and build larger resistance volumes with low risk of injury. There are 11 exercises to choose from (8 for the upper body and 3 for the lower body). All require that you use different angles and postures that are cross-specific to the angles and postures required to throw a baseball, field a baseball, swing a bat, or run. First let's look at the upper-body exercises; then we'll explore the lower-body exercises.

Body Work for Your Upper Body

Let your body provide the resistance for these exercises. The first four will be familiar to you from the flexing routines. You

---

*See chapter 9 for details about how to figure your resistance volume. For ease of body-work volume calculation, remember that in *horizontal* work when the feet are below the belly button (center of gravity), resistance is 60 percent of body weight. When feet are parallel with the belly button, resistance is 80 percent of body weight. When feet are above the belly button, resistance is 100 percent of body weight.

may or may not choose to use a riser or step for some of these exercises.

1. Elbow-ups are a scapular stabilizer. Perform sets of three to five reps with hands on thighs, with hands on belly button, with thumbs in armpits, and with hands behind head.

2. Forearm-ups are also a scapular stabilizer. Perform sets of three to five reps with forearms straight (fastball position), in (breaking-ball position), and out (change-up position).

3. Push-ups are great for reinforcing the Flex-T position. They are an elbow and shoulder joint integrity builder. Perform sets of three to five reps with hands forward (fastball position), hands out (change-up position), and hands in (breaking-ball position; see figure 5.1).

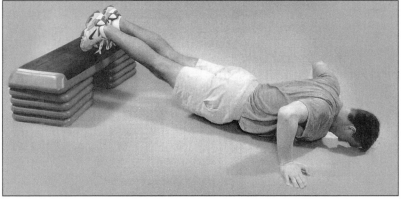

Figure 5.1   Push-ups with hands in the pronate position and feet on a riser.

If you can't do a regular push-up (with weight distributed from toes to palms of hands), do bent-knee type push-ups (with weight distributed from knees to palms of hands). When you change the angle of the hands, keep the elbows shoulder height in a Flex-T position. It isn't necessary to touch the chest to the floor during a push-up. This causes hyperflex and inefficient stresses in the shoulder. Maintain a stable pitching posture through the total range of motion.

4. Butt-ups are another elbow and shoulder joint integrity builder you might remember from your integrated flexing exercises. Perform sets of three to five reps with hands forward (fastball position), hands out (change-up position), hands in (breaking-ball position), and hands backward (also fastball position, see figure 5.2).

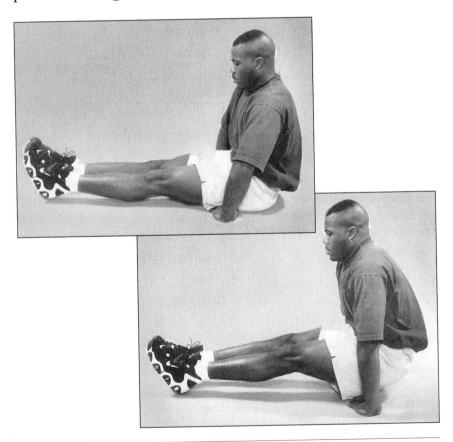

Figure 5.2   Butt-ups with hands in the supinate position.

5. Horizontal bench dips are a postural stabilizer and an elbow and shoulder joint integrity builder. Perform sets of three to five reps with heels of palms forward (fastball position), palms in (change-up position), heels of palms out (breaking-ball position), and heels of palms back (fastball position) at three different heights (to tolerance; see figure 5.3).

Figure 5.3 Horizontal bench dips.

For shoulder joint integrity, do not dip to where elbows bend below 90 degrees. It helps to look in a mirror at your technique while doing bench dips. Stabilize first; then lift up from the 90-degree angle established by the elbows. If it is too difficult to do bench dips between two benches (from heel to palms), put your feet on the ground as illustrated.

6. Horizontal chin-ups, pull-ups, palm-in ups, and palm-out ups (as shown in figure 5.4) are postural stabilizers and elbow and shoulder joint integrity builders.

Figure 5.4 Horizontal palm-out ups.

With horizontal chin-ups, lie underneath a squat rack with an Olympic bar across the rack and do the four angle pull-ups (palms forward, backward, in, and out) on the bar in a prone position with elbows in the Flex-T. Feet can be on the ground or on a bench level with or above belly-buttton height. Lift body, one set at each of four angles, three to five reps to tolerance.

7. Vertical dips: Perform sets of three to five reps with hands forward (fastball position), hands out (change-up position), hands in (breaking-ball position), and hands back (also fastball position) at three different foot heights (to tolerance; see figure 5.5). Never dip below 90 degrees at the elbows.

Figure 5.5 Vertical dips with hands in the supinate position.

With vertical dips and chin-ups, keep feet and legs in front of belly button (center of gravity) with head over torso and a firm posture through the lift. Do not sling your legs or swing your body to get this exercise going. Postural and scapular stabilization must be maintained. Never hang with arms in a straight position. (Hanging total body weight on the arms with chin-ups isolates tendons and ligaments. Stretching these tendons and ligaments in the elbow and shoulder can cause laxity in the joint. Once stretched out, connective tissue doesn't bounce back.) Always keep a little muscle flex in the elbow and shoulder joint. The goal is to achieve a strong body and stable shoulder joint.

If an athlete can do sets of 3 to 5 reps at four angles or 20 total chin-ups, he should do at least 28 dips, 7 reps at each of four angles (one-third more reps for balancing the backside).

8. Vertical chin-ups, pull-ups, palm-out ups, palm-in ups. If possible, perform sets of three to five reps at each of four angles for the ups.

Remember: Keep your feet and legs in front of your belly button (center of gravity) with head over torso and a firm posture through the lift. Do not sling your legs or swing your body to get going. Maintain postural and scapular stabilization. Always work between angles of 90 and 180 degrees.

Body Work for Your Lower Body

To work the lower body we'll add dumbbells for further resistance. Leg muscle systems are bigger and can stand a little more resistance. But don't overdo. Pitchers shouldn't use dumbbells heavier than 25 pounds with lunges, strides, step-ups, and step-downs. Body weight plus 50 pounds is plenty of resistance while maintaining balance through the movements. Remember to *always* move ball-of-foot to ball-of-foot with each exercise.

1. Dumbbell lunges forward and backward are a postural stabilizer; functional leg strength builder; and hip, knee, ankle integrity builder (see figure 5.6). Perform sets of three to five reps to tolerance.

Figure 5.6 Dumbbell lunges.

2. Dumbbell strides right and left are the same as lunges, only you add a torso rotation at the end of the motion. To train for hitting, you rotate and squat at stride-foot contact. Pitchers rotate and squat late at 75 percent of stride length. Perform sets of three to five reps to tolerance.

3. Dumbbell step-ups and step-downs are done on a box or a stair step. Face forward with the weights at your center of gravity; then step up onto the box or stair, and then step down. Perform this movement with your toes at three different angles: toes straight, toes in, and toes out. Then turn around with your back to the box or stair, and repeat the movement, stepping up *backwards*. Perform three to five reps at each toe angle (to tolerance).

Machine Work

Weight machines can further enhance upper-body trunk stabilization and scapular stabilization with appropriate positions and angles. In the next few pages I'll illustrate my favorite machine exercises for pitchers. Since each machine controls range of motion, you can concentrate on making the resistance as cross-specific as possible. In all the exercises, your forearm, hand, and wrist positions for fastballs, breaking balls, and change-ups become your training positions in the machine. For example, when you are working backside on the pec deck, the row machine, and reverse fly machine, find your Flex-T and work thumbs up, thumbs horizontal, and thumbs down to create different angles with wrist and forearm. In this way traditional machine work can be made to do skill-specific resistance training with appropriate postures, positions, and angles in each movement.

Machine Exercises for Your Upper Body

1. Pulley machine (one set of three to five reps at each of four angles—thumbs up, thumbs down, thumbs front, and thumbs back). See figure 5.7.

Figure 5.7 Pulley machine work. You may work standing upright or try variations like this, where you bend over. Start with arms in a Flex-T and cross over your body.

2. Pec deck machine (one set of three to five reps each with your wrists at three angles and your body facing away from the machine; then two sets of three to five reps at three angles facing toward the machine. Then one set with forearms stable at three angles and one set with forearms extending at three angles). See figure 5.8.

Figure 5.8 Pec deck.

3. Upright row machine (one set of three to five reps at each of four angles). See figure 5.9.
4. Reverse fly machine (one set of three to five reps at each of three angles).
5. Lat pull-down machine (one set of three to five reps at four angles). See figure 5.10.

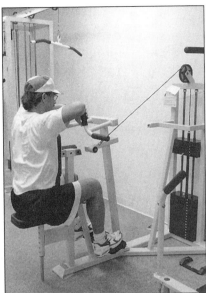

Figure 5.9 Upright row with hands in the pronate position.

Figure 5.10 A lat pull-down exercise with a narrow grip.

Machine Exercises for Your Lower Body

Four weight machines can further enhance lower-body strength and trunk stabilization:

1. Quad machine (one set, using both legs at the same time, three to five reps at each of three angles—linear, toes in, and toes out—to tolerance. See figure 5.11. Then one set of five reps at each of the three angles, alternating legs, each leg at one-half weight).

Figure 5.11 Quad machine.

2. Horizontal hamstring machine (one set, using both legs at the same time, three to five reps at each of three angles—linear, toes in, and toes out—to tolerance. Then one set of five reps at each of the three angles, alternating legs, each leg at one-half weight). See figure 5.12.

Figure 5.12 Hamstring machine.

3. Leg press machine (one set, pressing with both legs at the same time, three to five reps at each of three angles—linear, toes in, and toes out—to tolerance. Then one set of five reps at each of the three angles, alternating legs, each leg at one-half weight).

4. Calf machine (one set, using both legs at the same time, three to five reps at each of three angles—linear, toes in, and toes out—to tolerance. Then, one set of three to five reps at each of the three angles, alternating legs, each leg at one-half weight). Calf exercises can also be performed on the leg press machine (see figure 5.13).

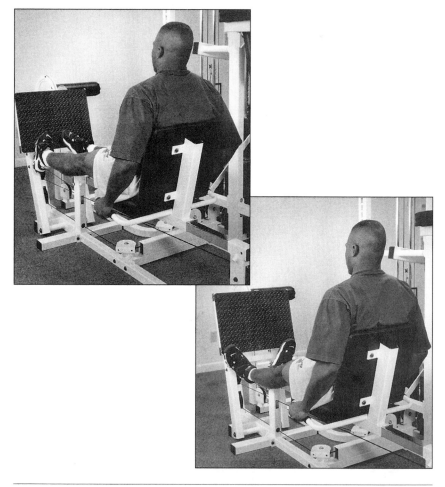

Figure 5.13   Toes-in and toes-out calf work on the leg press machine.

Heavy Weight Work

When athlete, coach, and strength trainer are convinced that a pitcher has peaked with all the light dumbbell, elastic cord, body work, and upper- and lower-body machine exercises, then heavier lift weight training with dumbbells, barbells, and machines are an option. Again, even with heavy resistance training, try to integrate, not isolate. Change body angle and position angles, but rotate only through a safe range of motion. With the barbells, work concentric and eccentric (against gravity and with gravity). On machines, change the angle of the parts you can't rotate. The heavier lifts are for heavier volume days and should be post-throwing days. When a pitcher isn't throwing off the mound (i.e., off-season), it is optimal to lift heavy, total body, two to three times per week. As an athlete gets into the season, a starting pitcher will lift heavy the same number of times he starts in a given week (i.e., if he has two starts per week then he will lift heavy twice per week, the day after he starts). A relief pitcher averaging four appearances per week will break his total lift volumes down into four submaximal workouts per week. In other words, match your lifting volumes and throwing volumes each week to be cross-specific.

Functional heavy weight training is prime-mover oriented with a cross-specific purpose—creating body positions that are skill-specific to throwing, then training to build strength and stability in those positions. Putting the total body in different postures and lifting with shoulder and elbow joints stabilized—while forearms and wrists alternate or move in linear (fastball), pronating (change-up), and supinating (breaking ball) angles—is proper heavy dumbbell protocol. Heavy barbell work precludes forearm and wrist rotation, and instead requires working from a stable posture and a stable Flex-T, cross-specific with pitching.

Heavy Weight Work for Your Upper Body

There are six basic heavy free-weight exercises to choose from:

1. Dumbbell press (one set of five reps at three angles in four postures).
   a. Standing—balls of feet shoulder width, knees flexed, head on line and in front of belly button, Flex-T with shoulders and elbows.
   b. On an incline—balls of feet broad base, Flex-T with shoulders and elbows.
   c. Horizontal—lie down on bench, balls of feet stabilized, Flex-T with shoulders and elbows.
   d. On a decline—Flex-T with shoulders and elbows, feet hooked to stabilize body. See figure 5.14.

Figure 5.14   Dumbbell press on a decline.

2. Lying-down triceps extensions, forearm press-ups (one set of 15 reps each). See figure 5.15.

Figure 5.15   Forearm press-ups.

3. Lawn mowers (one set of five reps at each of three angles—
   linear, pronate, and supinate—with both arms). See
   figure 5.16.

Figure 5.16 Lawn mowers.

4. Shrugs (one set of five reps at each of three angles—linear, forward and reverse). See figure 5.17.

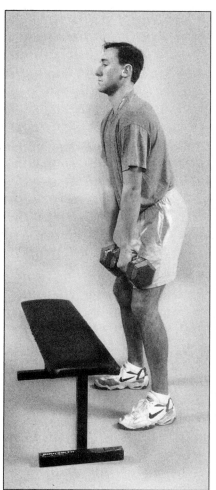

Figure 5.17   Shrugs.

5. Curl bar, one set of each (see figure 5.18 on next page).

   a. Biceps—three to five each
   b. Triceps—three to five each
   c. Standing triceps extensions—three to five each

Figure 5.18   Working with the curl bar.

6. Flex-T bench press (15 reps—never heavier than body weight; never let elbows get below Flex-T). See figure 5.19.

Figure 5.19   Flex-T bench press.

Heavy Weight Work for Your Lower Body

To work your lower body with heavy weights, I recommend returning to the weight machine exercises and adding more resistance so that you reach "burnout" at the fifth rep in each angle. Take a little more time between angle changes to lessen the intensity.

Training Summary

Properly implemented, conditioning workloads will create parity among connective tissue and muscles of all sizes. A pitcher will build functional strength with lean muscle mass, not bulk. Training will balance mechanical efficiency and throwing workloads in micro and macro cycles (see chapters 8 and 9). It will be cross-specific to skill development and, therefore, increase chances for success in competition. I bring up mechanical efficiency (skill) and throwing workloads for a reason. The next two chapters discuss throwing skill development, on flat ground and mound, to complement the physical conditioning discussed in this and the previous two chapters.

Flat-Ground Throwing

If throwing from a mound is a tearing-down process, why not skill train on flat ground?

Nolan Ryan

Good question! Nolan Ryan understood that the stresses on joints, connective tissues, and muscles are far greater when throwing down a slope. At Bio-Kinetics, we learned that the neuromuscular sequencing involved in pitching is exactly the same throwing on flat ground or a mound. Because of this, pitchers of all ages should learn and practice their skill in a progression that emphasizes more flat-ground training than mound training. *Both* are necessary, but coaches should structure workouts by practicing on flat ground and competing on a slope.

With this thought in mind, let's set a foundation for flat-ground throwing protocols that will skill train pitchers for competition. Pitching from the mound will be discussed in chapter 7.

Throwing Motion

The drills in this chapter and in chapter 7 are skill based. This is all well and good, but to have solid mechanics, you must practice solid mechanics. So, to make sure you get the most out of these drills, let's be clear about the fundamentals of throwing.

Throwing is a kinetic energy link, or sequential muscle loading, from ball-of-foot to ball-of-foot up through the body into release point. When a mechanically efficient pitcher initiates the throwing motion, his body strides ball-of-foot to ball-of-foot in four fluid phases. He goes from (1) dynamic balance (or absorbing energy), into (2) direction and (3) weight shift at footstrike into energy translation, and finally into (4) launch and release (or delivery of energy into the baseball).

1. Dynamic Balance

Dynamic balance is a different "teach" than what has been traditionally instructed. In an efficient pitching motion, there is no static, "stop-at-the-top" balance point. Laws of inertia tell us that once in motion an object tends to remain in motion. It's silly for a pitcher to actually *stop* for balance when he can be taught to *maintain* balance while initiating the momentum of his delivery into direction. This is a much more efficient way of turning potential energy into kinetic energy.

2. Direction

Kinetic energy is maximized by stabilizing body posture through body movement. Keeping eyes level to the horizon will help to stabilize the upper and lower body. When a pitcher's eyes stay level to the horizon, his head stays over the belly button, or center of gravity. If he is efficient going ball-of-foot to ball-of-foot as feet deliver torso, then within his body's musculoskeletal system (his closed chain) he should be better able to maintain trunk or postural stabilization in an efficient directional movement toward home plate. For shoulder joint integrity, the elbows, as the hands separate, should go down, out, and up and away from the body into a Flex-T; the elbows should never go behind the shoulder plane (hyperextension) during the lower body's ball-of-foot to ball-of-foot sequencing. Hyperextension creates misdirection of both potential and kinetic energy.

3. Weight Transfer

As the athlete strides into foot strike, the energy created by body weight, speed, distance of stride, and slope of mound will eventually stop going in that forward direction and translate up through the body into arms and baseball. The elbows should be at shoulder height and slightly in front of shoulder points (the Flex-T), lined up with hips and balls of feet, over a stable posture created by head and belly button. The forearms, both throwing side and front side, are along for the ride until torso rotation, when shoulders pass each other *late* into the delivery phase at about 75 percent of stride length.

4. Launch and Release

As the shoulders pass each other in this upper-body rotation, the arm slot (overhand, three-quarters, sidearm) should stay a consistent distance from the pitcher's head. His throwing forearm, wrist, and hand translate all the energy that comes from the feet through the body into the baseball by snapping straight into the launch and release. The energy flows through the middle finger into the middle of the baseball. After release, momentum carries the upper body forward. The arm decelerates in exactly the reverse sequence of acceleration, with the belly button, or center of gravity, over the landing knee. The head, torso, and ball of foot should be on line with the pitcher's target.

These mechanics are the same when playing catch, doing drills, or pitching. Here is the protocol I recommend to optimize skill training on flat ground. After athletes have taken the field, done their loosen-up and warm-up work (i.e., aerobic work, flexing, anaerobic plyometrics, or sprints), they should do the following:

- Short, medium, and long tosses, finishing with the hat drill (for throwing mechanics and throwing endurance).
- The towel drill (for pitching mechanics).
- The line drill (for practicing fastball, curveball, slider, and change-up release points).
- The football toss (for trunk and scapular stabilization). This one is optional.

Short, Medium, and Long Tosses, Finishing With the Hat Drill

In this drill, hold the number of throws constant, but let short-, medium-, and long-toss distance change as a function of the athlete's tolerance. (In other words, the day after an athlete pitches in a ball game, short, medium, and long toss may involve less overall distance than three days later when stiffness and soreness are not a factor.) The mechanical key to remember is that even for short, medium, and long tosses pitchers are still going ball-of-foot to ball-of-foot. They must still find a posture and keep that posture with their eyes level, separating hands, ball, and glove in a thumbs-under movement. This will get a pitcher into his Flex-T with elbows going out, up, and away from the body to shoulder height, slightly in front of shoulder points. When pitchers throw in these drills, they must be aggressive with their body and easy with their throwing arm (and *always* to tolerance). Understand that the arm is along for the ride. The energy generated by going ball-of-foot to ball-of-foot translates from the feet through the body into the arm, and works most efficiently with proper balance, posture, and joint integrity. Don't make it violent, and remember, never throw a baseball above head height on a baseball field—not in training, in rehab, or in game situations, and *always* work to tolerance.

As a healthy athlete, you should be able to throw 100 to 120 times on the flat ground in sets of 15, the final 30 with maximum effort at approximately 120 feet. Sets of 15 throws simulate 15 pitches per inning—the average major-league pitch total per inning (more cross-specific training). So, get a partner and start tossing to one another at about 30 to 60 feet apart for the first two short sets; then move about 30 feet farther apart for the two medium sets; and finally stand 120 feet apart for the last three to four sets. Use the one-hop hat drill that last set (see figure 6.1). Put your hat down in front of you and have your partner do the same. Then try to hit each other's hat. Throwing the ball 120 feet on one hop takes the same energy as lofting it 120 feet, but it better reinforces proper mechanics at release point.

Figure 6.1a   Short toss to tolerance.

Figure 6.1b-c   A series of tosses finishing with the hat drill.

If you're in rehab, working pain free with this volume of throws means that your throwing endurance, your muscular strength, and your mechanics have matched up to a point where you are physically ready for the mound (see chapter 10).

Flat-Ground Towel Drill

The towel drill is a simulation drill for windup and stretch mechanics, using a hand towel instead of a baseball through a full range of motion. Pair off into a thrower and a receiver. The thrower measures off his maximum stride and adds five feet. The receiving partner gets down on one knee and holds out his hand at the height of his pitching partner's belly button. The pitcher goes through his motion (windup and set position) with proper mechanics, ball-of-foot to ball-of-foot, posture stable, eyes level and on his partner's hand. His hands (one with glove and one with towel) separate, elbows up and out, into a Flex-T at front-foot contact. From this position, his torso will glide into late rotation with the forearm slapping his partner's hand with the towel. Do this drill to tolerance, in sets of 15: the first set from just the windup; the second set using the regular leg lift from the stretch; and the third set with the quick leg from the stretch.

Remember, ideal pitching mechanics require dynamic balance, postural stabilization, joint integrity with shoulders, elbows and head (i.e., Flex-T) and late rotation (where belly button, or center of gravity, gets to 75 percent of stride length before the torso rotates into launch and delivery). The beauty of the towel drill is that it teaches these perfect throwing mechanics without the physical wear and tear of throwing a baseball. Quite simply, if the pitcher misses striking his partner's hand either right or left, it is a posture change. If he misses short, it is a premature rotation. Figure 6.2 illustrates this drill and its application.

Figure 6.2   The towel drill on flat ground.

Line Drill

The line drill is a release-point drill. Pair off. One partner gets down like a catcher on flat ground about 45 feet away. The pitcher throws all of his pitches (fastball, curveball, slider, change-up) 15 pitches at a time from the windup and stretch (regular lift and quick leg). It is particularly good neuromuscular skill work to throw all pitches at less distance, alternating at 15-pitch intervals. Throwing fastballs for one interval, sliders for another, curves for a third, and change-ups for a fourth helps to groove the feel of your release point. Your partner can also use a hat or a towel for home plate to get a perspective on location.

Remember, distance magnifies mistakes, and the mound exacerbates both mistakes and mechanical inefficiencies. So timing and feeling the delivery on flat ground, at a shorter distance, is a proprioceptive skill drill that builds mental and physical confidence. Again, it does not stress the arm as much as throwing off the mound, even though the same energy links and sequential muscle loading takes place with each pitch.

Football Toss (Optional)

Throwing a football has caused some controversy within the baseball community, but it is a proven way to cross-train for strength and throwing mechanics. The football has been a very good teaching tool for me and the athletes whom I have worked with. At 13 ounces, a football builds strength by offering an overload situation with every throw. Mechanically, to make the football spiral, you have to go ball-of-foot to ball-of-foot with your eyes level and your elbows up and slightly in front of shoulder points (the Flex-T with trunk and scapular stabilization). However, the football is not to be thrown with an unhealthy arm and it is always thrown only to tolerance. Football tossing is more a tune-up or maintenance device for upper-body mechanics and strength, especially the Flex-T postural and scapular stabilization.

Put It ALL Together: The Elastic Cord Flex-T/Rotate Late Drill

Want an easy way to check on—or improve—your mechanics and increase your arm speed in the process? Then this drill is for you.

Equipment

You'll need an elastic cord at least as long as you measure from elbow to elbow when you assume the Flex-T position. You'll also use a ball and glove to perform the exercise outdoors.

Purpose

Primarily this drill will teach you the feel of the Flex-T and the appropriate late rotation that occurs after your front foot strike. It will also help you diagnose and correct mechanical flaws in your posture, Flex-T position, and follow through. Secondarily, this drill will improve your arm speed. The elastic cord gives your pitching motion added snap. After you take away the cord, your muscles will retain the "memory" of working through the motion at a slightly greater speed.

Procedure

Loop one end of the elastic cord and hook it around your pitching hand thumb. Give yourself an elbow to elbow expanse of cord and wrap the excess cord around the wrist of your glove hand. Then, if you are indoors, go through your pitching motion. Outdoors you should go ahead and throw a ball. Work on flat ground. If the cord touches your chest while you are in your Flex-T position, then you have drawn your elbows too far back. Adjust your Flex-T so the cord doesn't touch your chest.

Sequence

Perform this drill outside before short, medium, and long tosses. When you take this drill inside, work it in after your medicine ball exercises and before the towel drill.

Training Summary

I tell pitchers that the body was designed for work on flat ground. Flat-ground throwing is low-risk skill and endurance training. The logic is inescapable: Teach on flat ground; time it on the mound! Smart work preparation is just as important as hard work preparation.

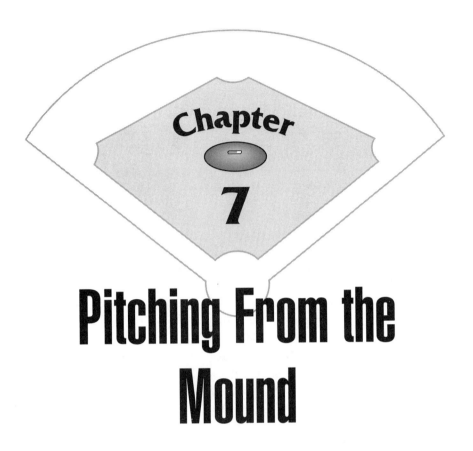

Chapter 7

Pitching From the Mound

When a pitcher steps on the mound, he literally and figuratively takes his body to another level of performance.

Matt Mitchell, PhD, sports psychologist, former PGA golfer

Once a solid physical and mechanical base has been established on flat ground, a pitcher can go to the mound with much more confidence. As I'll detail later in the chapter, skill-work protocols from the mound involve a five-step work progression:

1. Towel drill.
2. Front mound tosses or *downs*.
3. Back mound tosses or *ups*.
4. Back-to-front mound tosses or *ups and downs*.
5. Pitching off the rubber from windup and set positions at distance, to tolerance—a function of whether a pitcher is in rehab or prehab and where he is in his micro or macro cycle.

Throwing downhill off the mound is a tearing-down process, even with perfect mechanics and functional strength. Be conservative with pitch totals and intensity in preparation.

In each of the drills presented in this chapter, a coach must remind his pitcher to find a posture and keep it (usually, hitting posture and pitching posture are the same—this is a good "teach"), stride ball-of-foot to ball-of-foot, get elbows to a Flex-T, keep eyes level, and rotate late (at 75 percent of stride length). A coach's words must become a pitcher's *feel* for mechanical efficiency. Dynamic balance, weight transfer, postural stabilization, joint integrity, energy translation, late torso rotation, and forearm angle into launch are meaningless without kinesthetic awareness. Neither coach nor pitcher should ever put results ahead of mechanics. Use skill work to turn words and thoughts into a *feel* for a perfect motion.

In each of these drills, do everything in sets of 15, with a brief rest between each set, to simulate an inning pitched. The variations within each set are limitless. For example, in the towel drill a healthy pitcher could do 5 with a windup, 5 with a regular stretch, and 5 with a quick-step stretch. He can also vary the forearm angle to get the proper feel for fastball, breaking ball, and change-up release points. One 15-rep set, with the towel, in prehab allows more time for actually throwing the baseball. All pitchers are unique in the amount of time they need to spend working with the baseball and their release points. Rehabing pitchers will do more towels (three 15-rep sets: i.e., 15 with a windup, 15 with a regular stretch, and 15 with a quick-step stretch) and less baseball work because the towel, while reinforcing perfect mechanics is easier on the arm. Finally, as a rule, mound skills are learned quicker, with less risk of injury, when a pitcher throws fewer pitches more frequently. Now let's take a look at the five steps of the mound-drill progression:

Towel Drill

This is the same drill we did on flat ground (see pages 115-116) except hand strike is stride plus six of the pitcher's feet from where the lead foot contacts the mound. The extra distance is a concession to the slope of the mound. I like the drill to precede throwing so the pitcher's body can adjust to the mound without taking anything out of his arm. Repetitions and sets are optional, but 15 reps with any one type of delivery (wind up, stretch, quick-step stretch) is the optimal maximum for normal skill work.

Downs

Get into the stretch position in front of the rubber. Find a balanced posture, with your feet spread at shoulder width and your knees slightly flexed in an athletic position.* Start with your hands together on your chest. From this starting point, step behind with the posting foot, forward with the stride foot, break hands thumbs under, take elbows up into the Flex-T, rotate late, and deliver the ball (see figure 7.1). Make sure the posture is consistent and make sure that head and throwing forearm stay at the same angle and distance with torso rotation into launch. Throw the ball, to tolerance, 5 to 15 times.

---

*Flexing the knees creates a natural shock absorber. It helps balance and postural stabilization through weight transfer as the body moves down the mound to deliver the ball.

Figure 7.1   Downs.

Figure 7.1   *(continued)*

Ups

Get into the stretch position behind the mound on flat ground. Find a balanced posture, with your feet spread at shoulder width and your knees slightly flexed in an athletic position. Start with your hands together on your chest. From this starting point, step behind with the posting foot, forward with the stride foot, break hands thumbs under, take elbows up into the Flex-T, rotate late, and deliver the ball (see figure 7.2). Your front foot should actually be landing uphill. This forces your upper body to lean into the throw so elbows and forearms can create an angle at release point that will get the baseball to the catcher. This lean is a reinforcer for postural stabilization. Throw the ball, to tolerance, 5 to 15 times.

Figure 7.2 Ups.

Figure 7.2   *(continued)*

Ups and Downs

Get into the stretch position on the slope behind the rubber, with your front foot contacting the back side of the rubber. Use the same body position you did for your ups and your downs. From this starting point, lean into the slope, step behind with the posting foot, forward with the stride foot, break hands thumbs under, take elbows up into the Flex-T, rotate late, and deliver the ball (see figure 7.3). Be aggressive with the body going up and down the slope of the mound. The purpose of this drill is to teach dynamic balance and postural stabilization during a more intense movement. This up-the-mound-down-the-mound movement into launching the baseball is far more difficult than the actual windup and stretch—a perfect lead-in to just those movements. Throw the ball, to tolerance, 5 to 15 times.

Figure 7.3   Ups and downs.

Figure 7.3   *(continued)*

Windup and Stretch

Start skill-work pitching from the stretch position and finish skill-work pitching from the windup, to tolerance, in sets of 15 pitches. Try to keep total pitches between 45 and 60. Throw all pitches with perfect mechanics and low intensity. The windup is, basically, a step into the stretch position after a small weight shift from stride foot to post foot. All the mechanics of the previous exercises apply. The catcher should be down at whatever distance is comfortable for the pitcher. Pitch selection should also be worked on in sets of 15. Practice fastball, curveball, slider, and change-up to simulate game conditions. Remember that no pitch thrown with proper mechanical efficiency puts any more stress on the arm than any other pitch.

Training Summary

As coach and athlete work, the daily number of throws can be baselined as a benchmark for quantifying progress in each pitcher's preparation (prehab or rehab). Intensity is always a variable—a function of the athlete's daily tolerance. I can't emphasize enough that skill work should be perfect, low-intensity work. The body will not forget how to throw hard, but it will learn how to throw inefficiently if you let it. Strive for the feel of a perfect delivery—save high intensity and hard throwing for competition.

Part II

Fit to Pitch Training Program

In chapter 3, I quoted Nolan Ryan about a baseball season being like a marathon. His intuition was both country smart and correct—sport science is proving it! From spring training to the World Series, a season is broken down into individual games. The team schedule, like the distance of a marathon, is predictable. But every mile in a marathon is different and so is every game in a season. The athlete's physical response to each game (or mile) is also different. His response is a function of mechanical efficiency, physical conditioning, and throwing workload, integrated with how he's prepared for the long and short of a season. By definition, the long of a season is his macro cycle; the short of a season is his micro cycle. Integrating the preparation for micro and macro cycles is the foundation for part II and a fit to pitch program for pitchers of all ages and ability levels.

I'll take all the components from chapters 2 to 7—flexibility, stamina, endurance, and prime-mover training plus flat-ground and mound-skill drills—and show you how to develop a personalized macro cycle (yearlong) program in chapter 8 and a personalized micro cycle (game-to-game) program in chapter 9. In chapter 8 you'll see that a macro cycle is a pitcher's yearlong adaptation to skill, strength, and throwing stress. Chapter 9 will show you how a pitcher repairs and then prepares between appearances.

Chapter 8

The Macro Cycle

There is a fine line between ritual and routine. Ritual is work without knowing the reason. Routine is reasonable work for a desired result.

Len Sakata, former major-league infielder, coach, Chiba Lotte Marines, Japan

In preceding chapters, I've talked about cross-training with conditioning and mechanics and how it relates to a pitcher's micro and macro training cycles. A macro cycle is the sum total of all the training and competing a pitcher does from the start of the season until its end. (Page 135 provides you with an illustration of the time and variables involved in the macro cycle.) Micro cycles comprise the work a pitcher does game-to-game and between some performances during the season. However, the concepts of tolerance and wound healing, the variability of volume load, frequency, intensity, and duration and rehabilitation or prehabilitation must also be taken into account when examining a pitcher's micro and macro cycles. This chapter provides you with a cookbook or broad application of how all these concepts, variables, and factors can be integrated into the two cycles.

The variables involved in pitching are infinite and far too complex to control totally. An efficient training program, however, will integrate and manage those variables a pitcher can control. Coach, athlete, and trainer should be aware that any training program must continually match physical recovery with physical preparation for peak performance in competition. The bulk of that information will be discussed in chapter 9. For now, let's integrate both cycles in an overview.

The Macro Cycle

The function of the macro cycle is to train for physical recovery. A pitcher is wound healing from his initial pitch off a mound in spring to his final pitch off a mound in the championship game at season's end. How badly he "wounds" himself pitching is a function of his strength base (from off-season conditioning and in-season maintenance), his pitching mechanics, and the number of pitches he throws off a mound with intensity. How quickly and effectively a pitcher recovers is a function of blood chemistry, blood flow, aerobic capacity, stress management (mental and physical), and the depth of his muscle failure.

The macro cycle described in table 8.1 represents the general workout plan for the entire season. The plan integrates all the training protocols we've discussed thus far. You'll see, however, that this is only a general plan, because (barring injury) the macro cycle is composed of a season's worth of micro cycles that must each prepare a pitcher for his next appearance. As we will see, micro cycles need to be highly individualized.

The Macro Cycle: A Pitcher's Yearlong Adaptation to Skill, Strength, and Throwing Stress

The Macro Cycle Performance Timeline

A function of:
- Mechanical conditioning (skill)
- Physical conditioning (strength)
- Throwing conditioning (stress through pitching)

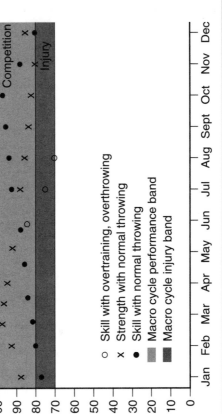

- ○ Skill with overtraining, overthrowing
- × Strength with normal throwing
- ● Skill with normal throwing
- ▨ Macro cycle performance band
- ▨ Macro cycle injury band

Givens*

- Pitchers will lose 20% of functional strength from April to October, even at normal workloads.
- Pitchers will increase their skill mechanics 20% from April to October unless they overdo their throwing workloads.

Indicators of Macro Cycle Program Problems*

- Inconsistent velocity with fastball
- Overall loss of velocity with fastball
- Loss of control with all pitches
- Joint stiffness; difficulty getting arm loose; dead arm
- Pain; inability to pitch

*Per studies conducted over 10 years at Bio-Kinetics.

Table 8.1   Macro-Cycle Overview

Type of work	Frequency	Intensity	Volume
Conditioning			
Aerobic and anaerobic work	Daily	To tolerance	Varies depending on what point pitcher is in on micro cycle
Body work	Daily	To tolerance	Varies depending on what point pitcher is in on micro cycle
Machine and free-weight work	Day after pitching (i.e., same as a pitcher's mound work frequency)	To tolerance	Varies depending on what point pitcher is in on micro cycle
Skill work (throwing)			
Flat-ground throwing (short, medium, and long tosses)	Daily	To tolerance	
Flat-ground towel drills	Daily	To tolerance (especially in rehab situations)	
Flat-ground line drills	Optional—work on a need-to basis		
Flat-ground football tosses	Optional		
Mound work towel drills	Optional in prehab, mandatory in rehab		
Mound work—downs, ups, and ups & downs	Scheduled around game work	Low intensity, to tolerance	
Mound work from the stretch and windup	Scheduled around game work	Low intensity, to tolerance	

The following reminders are important when considering the macro cycle:

- All conditioning work is total body integration work; no isolation is allowed.
- All conditioning work will train right and left sides equally, back side one-third more in volume than front side to accommodate the excess stresses involved in decelerating the arm after the body has traveled down the mound.
- All conditioning work will be position specific, resistance specific, and/or movement specific to the skill of throwing and/or pitching.
- All conditioning work will relate reps per set to the number of pitches per inning at 15 to 20.
- All throwing work requires a neuromuscular sequencing of dynamic balance, bent-knee ball-of-foot to ball-of-foot weight transfer, postural and scapular stabilization, Flex-T elbow positioning, late torso rotation at 75 percent of stride length, head and eyes on line with center of gravity and balls of feet, and throwing forearm angle consistent with posture and head angle into launch and release.
- Throwing work is always skill work on both flat ground and on the mound: It should be perfect work, to tolerance. Don't put results ahead of mechanics until the skill, or the right feeling, has been mastered.

The Micro Cycle

The purpose of the micro cycle is to prepare a pitcher for his next appearance. This cycle takes a pitcher who is worn down from his last game and builds him up for his next. Most starters will pitch a game to the point of muscle failure. But every pitcher pays a different price, physically, to deliver a baseball. Because of this, muscle failure is hard to quantify. We do know that it takes about 72 hours to recover from the lactic acid buildup and the mini-tears in soft tissue caused by pitching to muscle failure. Generally, a reasonably conditioned, mechanically efficient *starting* pitcher *begins* to experience muscle failure at about 75 pitches *if* he gets there in 15- to 20-pitch innings (frequency and intensity). Muscle failure, however, can occur in as few as 35 pitches if he throws all these pitches in one inning!

A reasonably conditioned, mechanically efficient *relief* pitcher should be able to throw 75 game pitches in any 72-hour period before approaching muscle failure, with recovery time inversely proportionate to how he reached his 75 pitches. For example, if he throws 75 pitches over three days at 25 pitches per game, he should need only one day to recover. Seventy-five pitches over two days at 37 pitches per game would require two recovery days, and so on. Also, pregame mound pitches can be a factor for both starter and reliever. Try to minimize them. Starters should be able to warm up in 45 or fewer; relievers in 15 to 20. (This should be no problem if all pitchers loosen up to warm up to compete.)

The transition from physical recovery to physical preparation begins immediately after a pitcher leaves the game. If the pitcher is in muscle failure, he should ice and bike (or an equivalent aerobic activity) to stop the bleeding from mini-tears and flush lactic acid. Postgame nutrition (blood chemistry) should be protein oriented to enhance the building/ rebuilding process (a complete nutritional workup will be provided in chapter 11). Table 8.2 provides a micro-cycle overview for a typical starter in a five-man rotation.

Training Summary

You have now seen the many choices available in an integrated training program for pitchers. If we go back to the cookbook analogy, it is a pretty large cookbook. There are many training recipes to choose from. Coach and athlete must experiment, try different recipes, create different menus, determine likes

Table 8.2   Micro-Cycle Overview (For Starting Pitchers[a])

Days after game	Conditioning	Skill work
Day 1	Total body aerobic and anaerobic resistance training.	Flat-ground work, to tolerance.
Day 2[b]	Total body aerobic and anaerobic resistance training; light to medium resistance; no heavy machines or free weights for power pitchers; heavy machines or free-weight work is optional for finesse pitchers.	Flat-ground work, to tolerance; mound work to tolerance for power pitchers.
Day 3[b]	Total body aerobic and anaerobic resistance training; no heavy machines or free weights for finesse pitchers; heavy machines or free-weight work is optional for power pitchers.	Flat-ground work, to tolerance; mound work to tolerance for finesse pitchers.
Day 4	Total body aerobic and anaerobic training; light volumes of resistance training (primarily elastic cord work and light dumbbell work at 60%—aim for a mental and physical "feel good" tolerance).	Low intensity flat-ground work.
Day 5 (game day)	A little of everything to loosen up to warm up to compete.	

[a]Relievers who haven't gotten into games, or who only warmed up to go into a game (i.e., a "scare") should do a little mound work every other day to tolerance as a function of the workloads they sustained in their last game.

[b]Power pitchers need extra recovery time on days leading into a new start. Finesse pitchers need skill work closer to a new start (to reinforce the feel and command for their pitches). So power pitchers are on the mound at day 2. Finesse pitchers are on the mound at day 3. This changes as the season progresses because recovery takes longer late in the season; conversely, skill has been reinforced by the season's duration and finesse pitchers should require only a minimal tune-up between starts.

and dislikes, find what works and what doesn't. Training, like taste, is different for every pitcher. Everyone has to eat, just as everyone has to train, but don't be afraid to try different combinations. Remember, even Betty Crocker burns a brownie once in awhile. The key is not burning the whole batch, or letting one charred brownie spoil a whole meal. Now that you have an overview, you'll see in chapter 9 typical menus, or preparation protocols, for a starting pitcher and a reliever in their micro cycles.

The Micro Cycle

Don't confuse hard work with smart work. Plan your training around your game work *and* your recovery cycle.

Dr. John Gleddie, Canadian Olympic rowing consultant

Before I quantify and detail a couple of typical between-game workouts, I need to qualify the purpose of a between-game workout routine. In my coaching travels around the world, I have seen between-game workouts take on a mystical quality for some pitchers, a manic quality for other pitchers, and a moronic quality for still others. The key for mind and body integration is committing to a routine without getting too rigid.

What is too rigid? It is when a routine starts controlling the pitcher instead of the other way around. There must be some cognitive evaluation of body, time, effort, and task before every workout. It is the consistency of daily work that counts, not the performance of the same workout each day. It is good to find something that works and work at it purposefully, but it is just as important to find variations on that theme to avoid mind burnout and body boredom (i.e., neural stagnation). Pages 143 to 146 outline the cognitive base for the why, when, how, and what of a pitcher's pitching, repairing, and preparing program.

Apart from keeping a workout routine from becoming too rigid, individual micro-cycle workouts can also be qualified depending on

- whether the pitcher is a starter or reliever (that is, how much and how often the pitcher works),
- whether the pitcher is a power or finesse pitcher,
- the pitcher's functional strength,
- the pitcher's mechanical efficiency, and
- the tolerance, or intensity, at which a pitcher prefers to train.

So much for qualifying. Now it's time to put together everything we've discussed in the previous chapters to design and quantify some effective micro-cycle workouts. First, I'll show you how to determine a minimum training workload for a typical micro cycle. Then, I'll provide an example of a middle-of-the-road, between-game workout for a starting pitcher in a five-day rotation. Then I'll show you a reliever's micro-cycle workout. If you study these examples carefully, you'll be ready to design effective micro cycles for yourself. Use the blank forms in the appendix to formulate your own micro-cycle workouts.

The Why, When, How, and What of Training

Why pitchers train—overcompensation

Precision monitoring of the adaptation cycle allows prediction of the physiological recovery peak and the ideal performance state.

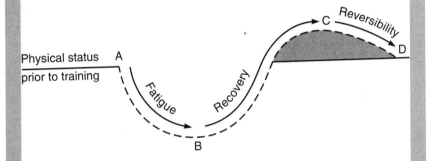

A: A pitching load is imposed.

- Fatigue builds during training.

B: The training session finishes.

- The recovery process begins.
- The body starts to rebuild all those constituents depleted during the training session.

C: Ideal performance peak for new pitching load.

- The body has restored all of its resources, and has, through a process called overcompensation, built up more constituents than were previously in the body.
- Enough time must be given to achieve overcompensation.

D: With no further stimulation, the body's reserve levels revert to their original levels.

When to train

Recognizing the individual recovery cycles informs the pitching coach of the arm fitness of the pitcher and helps prevent injury by unintentional overloading and by differentiating normal wear and tear from breakdown or injury.

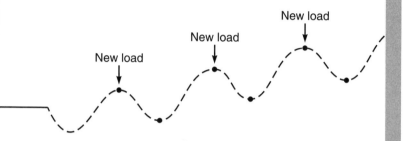

- Optimal training is realized when a new pitching load is imposed at the end of the recovery/overcompensation phase.
- The body does not become fitter during the training phase.
- The body adapts and overcompensates during the recovery phase.
- The training load merely activates the overcompensation process.
- The training load is not an end in itself.
- Maximizing overcompensation is the objective.
- The art of training is therefore mastering the timing of the *recovery* cycle.

How hard to train—intensity versus tolerance

The rigorous schedule does not allow for strength gains during the season. The objective is to minimize the strength loss by accurately managing the workload and recovery phase.

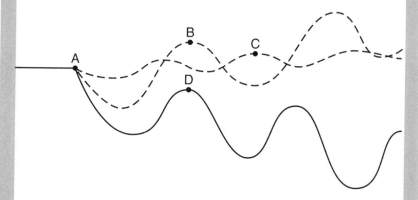

A: Start training.

- Do a cross-specific combination of skill training and resistance training.

B: Use an optimal load—neither too hard nor too easy.

- Overcompensation realizes reasonable gains.

C: If the load is too easy or too light

- overcompensation occurs but athlete realizes only moderate gain, and
- gains will take longer to occur but will be stable.

D: If the load is too heavy or the recovery phase too short, athlete will

- be prone to chronic fatigue or overtraining,
- have a predisposition to injury, and
- experience a performance decline.

What pitchers train for—long-term adaptation

With the knowledge of the individual adaptation to load recovery as it relates to performance in the developing pitcher, talent development can be more predictable and can become more efficient.

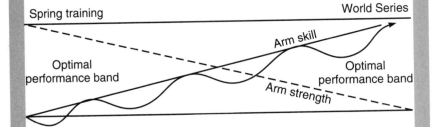

- Cycles can work over shorter or longer periods.
- Cycles are not always as regular as one might hope.
- The body's ability to adapt to a certain training load is often specific to the individual and has a unique time frame.
- The body adapts best to training loads that are cyclical, varied, and progressive—to tolerance.

Quantifying Your Weekly Throwing Load

The first step in the quantification process starts with determining weekly throwing workload volumes. This is figured for mound work only, and it becomes the *minimum* volume for weekly resistance-training workload. There is no functional maximum; the only constraints are genetics, tolerance, and motivation. If you have read my book *The Pitching Edge*, you will recognize the throwing workload formula:

$$\text{\# of pitches} \times \text{velocity}^2 \times \frac{.01}{\substack{\text{resistance} \\ \text{factor}}} \times \frac{1}{\substack{\text{mechanical} \\ \text{efficiency}}} = \substack{\text{minimum necessary} \\ \text{foot-pounds of work} \\ \text{per micro cycle}}$$

Note. Mechanical efficiency parameters have been determined by motion analysis at Bio-Kinetics, Inc. Most professional pitchers throw at 90-plus percent efficiency. Most amateur pitchers throw with at least 80 percent efficiency. Unless you get an accurate analysis, err on the side of modesty and assume you are less efficient than you probably are. This will cause a workload volume error on the plus side.

This formula is not perfect. It does give a numerical constant to build forward to, or backward from, as micro cycles become macro cycles.

A Micro Cycle for a Starter: Two Games in Seven Days

Assume our starting pitcher is a 200-pound power pitcher, with a 90-mile-per-hour fastball and a mechanical efficiency of 88 percent. We will pick up his micro cycle on game day with his pregame mound warm-up. (The only pregame resistance work we would do is dumbbells and cord to tolerance, a *max* of 2,100 pounds.)

Game Day (Sunday):

Throwing work volumes

Pregame mound work	50 pitches
Game 7 1/3 innings	130 pitches
Total	180 pitches

Workload = $180 \times 90 \text{ mph}^2 \times .01 \times \dfrac{1}{.88}$ = **16,660+ ft-lbs**

Post game ice & aerobic work

Stationary bike	30 minutes
Ice shoulder	20 minutes
Ice elbow	10 minutes

(less ice time for elbow because less muscle tissue)

Day 1 (Monday):

Day 1 is a day of heavy resistance work and light throwing (note how the work volumes break out).

Conditioning and resistance work volumes

Healthrider	15 minutes	
Aerobic work	30 minutes	
Integrated flexibility work		
Elastic cord work (light)		
8 exercises, 15 reps/exercise, 3 angles, 5 reps/angle	=	1,200 *
Light dumbbells (5 lbs)		
12 exercises, 15 reps/exercise, 3 angles, 5 reps/angle	=	900
Body work (feet elevated to tolerance)		
11 exercises, 15-20 reps/exercise, 3-4 angles, 5 reps/angle	=	26,400
Machine work (to tolerance)		
9 exercises, 15-20 reps/exercise, 3-4 angles, 5 reps/angle	=	10,100
Heavy free-weight work (to tolerance)		
6 exercises, 15-20 reps/exercise, 3-4 angles, 5 reps/angle	=	5,400
Total lbs		**44,000**

*See *The Pitching Edge* for information on how to arrive at these resistance figures.

Anaerobic work

8-12 minutes

Throwing work volumes

Short, medium, long toss to tolerance, 15-20 each distance
No drill work, no skill work

Total lbs   0

Day 2 (Tuesday):

Day 2 is a day of light resistance work and medium to heavy throwing. Remember if we were designing a micro cycle for a power pitcher, he would do mound skill work on day 2 after a start. A finesse pitcher would do mound skill work on day 3 after a start (see the micro cycle overview table in chapter 8).

Conditioning and resistance work volumes

Healthrider	15 minutes	
Aerobic work	30 minutes	
Integrated flexibility work		
Elastic cord work (light)		
8 exercises, 15 reps/exercise, 3 angles, 5 reps/angle	=	1,200
Light dumbbells (5 lbs)		
12 exercises, 15 reps/exercise, 3 angles, 5 reps/angle	=	900
Body work (feet elevated to tolerance)		
11 exercises, 15-20 reps/exercise, 3-4 angles, 5 reps/angle		= 19,800
Machine work (optional)	=	0
No heavy free weights	=	0

Total lbs   21,900

Anaerobic work

8-12 minutes

Throwing work volumes

Short, medium, long toss to tolerance
    15-20 short
    15-20 medium
    15-20 long

Towel drill windup/stretch (optional)
   15 windup
   15 stretch
Line drill windup/stretch (optional)
   15 windup FB, CB, CH
   15 stretch FB, CB, CH
Downs, ups, ups and downs
   15 downs
   15 ups
   15 ups and downs
Skill work windup/stretch (60 pitches)
   15 FB
   15 CB
   15 CH
   15 mix and match

$$\text{Workloads} = 60 \times 90 \text{ mph}^2 \times .01 \times \frac{1}{.88} = \textbf{5,533 lbs}$$

Day 3 (Wednesday)

Day 3 is a day of medium to heavy resistance work and medium to light throwing.

Conditioning and resistance work volumes

Healthrider	15 minutes	
Aerobic work	30 minutes	
Integrated flexibility work		
Elastic cord work (light)		
8 exercises, 15 reps/exercise, 3 angles, 5 reps/angle	=	1,200
Light dumbbells (10 lbs)		
12 exercises, 9 reps/exercise, 3 angles, 3 reps/angle	=	900
Body work (feet elevated to tolerance)[a]		
11 exercises, 15-20 reps/exercise, 3-4 angles, 5 reps/angle	=	19,800
Machine work (feet elevated to tolerance)[a]		
9 exercises, 15-20 reps/exercise, 3-4 angles, 5 reps/angle	=	10,100

[a] *Options:* For the body work, machine work, and heavy free-weight work protocols, a pitcher can work more volume with one protocol and back off on the other two or he can work any combination of the three exercises that feels right. In this case, the pitcher chose to perform body work and machine work, but chose not to work with free weights.

Heavy free-weight work (to tolerance)
  6 exercises, 15-20 reps/exercise, 3-4 angles,   =   0
    5 reps/angle

                                          Total lbs   32,000

Anaerobic work

8-12 minutes

Throwing work volumes

Short, medium, long toss to tolerance
  15-20 short
  15-20 medium
  15-20 long
Towel drill (optional)
Line drill (optional)
No skill work off mound

                                          Total lbs   0

Day 4 (Thursday)

Day 4 is a day of light resistance work and light throwing.

Conditioning and resistance work volumes

Healthrider   15 minutes
Aerobic work   30 minutes
Integrated flexibility work
Elastic cord work (light)
  8 exercises, 15 reps/exercise, 3 angles, 5 reps/angle   = 1,200
Light dumbbells (3 lbs)
  12 exercises, 9 reps/exercise, 3 angles, 3 reps/angle   =   900
Body work (feet elevated to tolerance)
  11 exercises, 9-12 reps/exercise, 3-4 angles,   = 19,800
    3-4 reps/angle
Machine work (optional)   =   0
No heavy free weights   =   0

                                          Total lbs   21,900

Anaerobic work

8-12 minutes

Throwing work volumes

Short, medium, long toss to tolerance
    15-20 short
    15-20 medium
    15-20 long
Towel drill (optional)
Line drill (optional)
No mound work   0

                                   Total lbs   0

Game Day (Friday, second start of the week)

Game day is a day for very light resistance work and very heavy throwing work. Do all normal pre-throwing work, but do it with low intensity. Save intense throwing for the game.

Conditioning and resistance work volumes

Healthrider	5 minutes	
Aerobic work	5 minutes	
Integrated flexibility work to tolerance		
Elastic cord work (light)		
8 exercises, 15 reps/exercise, 3 angles, 5 reps/angle	=	1,200 (max)
Light dumbbells (weight to tolerance)		
12 exercises, 9 reps/exercise, 3 angles, 3 reps/angle	=	900
Body work (optional)	=	0
Machine work (optional)	=	0
No heavy free-weight work	=	0

                                   Total lbs   **2,100**

Anaerobic work

None—perform light sprints

Throwing work volumes

Short, medium, long toss to tolerance
Downs, ups, ups and downs to tolerance

Pregame	55 pitches
Game 8 innings	136 pitches
Total	191 pitches

$$\text{Workload} = 191 \times 90 \text{ mph}^2 \times .01 \times \frac{1}{.88} = \textbf{17,600 ft-lbs}$$

Day 6 (Saturday)

The whole process of repairing and preparing to pitch starts over again.

Conditioning & resistance work volumes

Healthrider	15 minutes	
Aerobic work	30 minutes	
Integrated flexibility work		
Elastic cord work (light)		
8 exercises, 15 reps/exercise, 3 angles, 5 reps/angle	=	1,200
Light dumbbells (5 lbs)		
12 exercises, 15 reps/exercise, 3 angles, 5 reps/angle	=	900
Body work (feet elevated to tolerance)		
11 exercises, 15-20 reps/exercise, 3-4 angles, 5 reps/angle	=	26,400
Machine work (to tolerance)		
9 exercises, 15-20 reps/exercise, 3-4 angles, 5 reps/angle	=	10,100
Heavy free-weight work (to tolerance)		
6 exercises, 15-20 reps/exercise, 3-4 angles, 5 reps/angle	=	5,400
	Total lbs	**44,000**

Anaerobic work

8-12 minutes

Throwing work volumes

Short, medium, long toss to tolerance, 15-20 each distance
No drill work, no skill work

Total lbs	0

Seven-Day Workload Totals

Over the seven-day micro cycle, this power pitcher performed 168,000 pounds of conditioning volume work (and most of it—112,200 pounds—was low-risk body work!). He performed 39,793 pounds of mound-throwing work. In other words, he strength trained a 77,907-pound cushion which acts as a conditioning volume insurance policy against the wear and tear of current and future mound work. Too much? Maybe, maybe not. It's a micro cycle to be monitored as his seasonal macro cycle continues.

Day	Conditioning volume	Throwing volume
Sunday	2,100	16,660 (from the game)
Monday	44,000	0
Tuesday	21,900	5,533 (from skill work)
Wednesday	32,000	0
Thursday	21,900	0
Friday	2,100	17,600 (from the game)
Saturday	44,000	0
Totals:	168,000 lbs	39,793 lbs

If you want to see what this micro cycle would look like from soft tissue inside a pitcher's arm, check out pages 155-158, which depict thermographic scans showing the repairing and preparing process of Nolan Ryan's arm on a five-day micro cycle.

A Micro Cycle for a Reliever

A middle reliever appearing three days per week or a short reliever throwing five days per week would work the same routines, but in the medium or light resistance workload modes three to five days a week. For example, assume our reliever is also a 200-pound power pitcher with a 90-mile-per-hour fastball and a mechanical efficiency of 88 percent. Let's pick up his micro cycle on the same "game day" as our starter, figuring he came in and finished the last 1 2/3 innings of that Sunday's game.*

---

*A reliever's pregame drills are the same, to tolerance, as a starter's, except that more of them are optional on a need-to basis because he has more mound frequency.

Nolan Ryan—Repairing and Preparing to Pitch Through the Micro Cycle

In the following pages you'll see illustrations based on thermographic imaging of Nolan Ryan's right arm as he progresses through a micro cycle. As you look at the images, understand that the darker the shading, the more damaged the soft tissue. Accompanying each image is the date in the micro cycle (the day after the game is called "Game day +1," for instance) and a brief description of the training Nolan did. As you watch the shading on the images get lighter as game day approaches, I think you'll gain an appreciation of how the soft tissues repair from the last outing and prepare for the next.

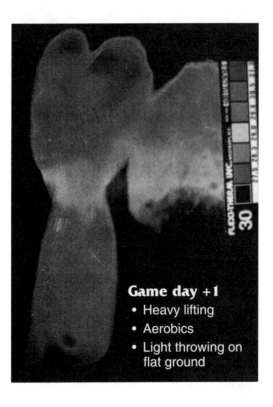

Game day +1
- Heavy lifting
- Aerobics
- Light throwing on flat ground

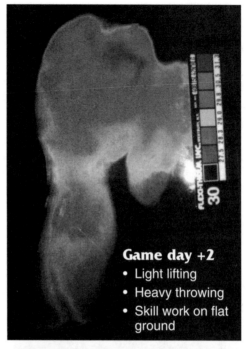

Game day +2
- Light lifting
- Heavy throwing
- Skill work on flat ground

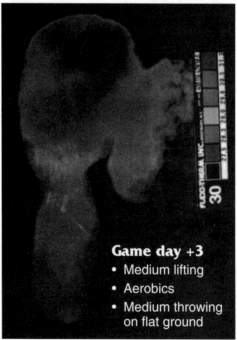

Game day +3
- Medium lifting
- Aerobics
- Medium throwing on flat ground

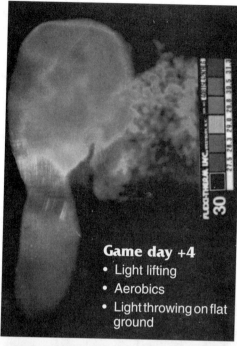

Game day +4
- Light lifting
- Aerobics
- Light throwing on flat ground

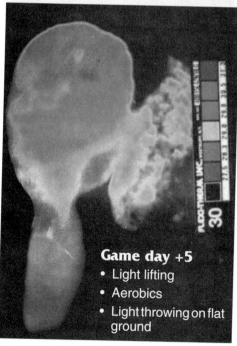

Game day +5
- Light lifting
- Aerobics
- Light throwing on flat ground

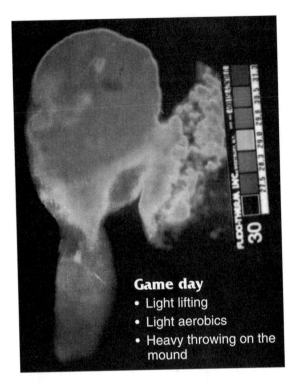

Game day
- Light lifting
- Light aerobics
- Heavy throwing on the mound

Game Day (Sunday)

Throwing work volumes

Bullpen warm-up and mound work	30 pitches
Game 1 2/3 innings	25 pitches
Total	55 pitches

$$\text{Workload} = 55 \times 90 \text{ mph}^2 \times .01 \times \frac{1}{.88} = \mathbf{5{,}062 \text{ ft-lbs}}$$

Conditioning and resistance work volumes

Healthrider	15 minutes	
Aerobic work	30 minutes	
Integrated flexibility work		
Elastic cord work (light)		
8 exercises, 15 reps/exercise, 3 angles, 5 reps/angle	=	1,200
Light dumbbells (10 lbs)		
12 exercises, 9 reps/exercise, 3 angles, 3 reps/angle	=	900
Body work (feet elevated to tolerance)[a]		
11 exercises, 15-20 reps/exercise, 3-4 angles, 5 reps/angle	=	19,800
Machine work (feet elevated to tolerance)[a]		
9 exercises, 15-20 reps/exercise, 3-4 angles, 5 reps/angle	=	10,100
Heavy free-weight work (to tolerance)[a]		
6 exercises, 15-20 reps/exercise, 3-4 angles, 5 reps/angle	=	0
Total lbs		**32,000**

[a] *Options:* For the body work, machine work, and heavy free-weight work protocols, a pitcher can work more volume with one protocol and back off on the other two or he can work any combination of the three exercises that feels right. In this case, the pitcher chose to perform body work and machine work, but chose not to work with free weights.

Day 2 (Monday)

Throwing work volumes

Bullpen warm-up mound work   35 pitches
No game

$$\text{Workload} = 35 \times 90 \text{ mph}^2 \times .01 \times \frac{1}{.88} = \mathbf{3,221 \text{ ft-lbs}}$$

Conditioning and resistance work volumes

Healthrider	15 minutes		
Aerobic work	30 minutes		
Integrated flexibility work			
Elastic cord work (light)			
8 exercises, 15 reps/exercise, 3 angles, 5 reps/angle		=	1,200
Light dumbbells (5 lbs)			
12 exercises, 15 reps/exercise, 3 angles, 5 reps/angle		=	900
Body work (feet elevated to tolerance)			
11 exercises, 15-20 reps/exercise, 3-4 angles,		=	19,800
5 reps/angle			
Machine work (optional)		=	0
No heavy free weights		=	0
		Total lbs	**21,900**

Day 3 (Tuesday)

Throwing work volumes

No mound work

	Total lbs	0

Conditioning and resistance work volumes

Healthrider	5 minutes		
Aerobic work	5 minutes		
Integrated flexibility work to tolerance			
Elastic cord work (light)			
8 exercises, 15 reps/exercise, 3 angles, 5 reps/angle		=	1,200 (max)
Light dumbbells (weight to tolerance)			
12 exercises, 9 reps/exercise, 3 angles, 3 reps/angle		=	900
Body work (optional)		=	0

Machine work (optional)	=	0
No heavy free-weight work	=	0

	Total lbs	**2,100**

Day 4 (Wednesday)

Throwing work volumes

Bullpen warm-up mound work	=	40 pitches
Game 2 1/3 innings	=	35 pitches
	Total	75 pitches

$$\text{Workload} = 75 \times 90 \text{ mph}^2 \times .01 \times \frac{1}{.88} = \textbf{6,903 ft-lbs}$$

Conditioning and resistance work volumes

Healthrider	15 minutes	
Aerobic work	30 minutes	
Integrated flexibility work		
Elastic cord work (light)		
8 exercises, 15 reps/exercise, 3 angles, 5 reps/angle	=	1,200
Light dumbbells (5 lbs)		
12 exercises, 15 reps/exercise, 3 angles, 5 reps/angle	=	900
Body work (feet elevated to tolerance)		
11 exercises, 15-20 reps/exercise, 3-4 angles, 5 reps/angle	=	19,800
Machine work (optional)	=	0
No heavy free weights	=	0

	Total lbs	**21,900**

Day 5 (Thursday)

Throwing work volumes

No mound work

	Total lbs	**0**

Conditioning and resistance work volumes

Healthrider	15 minutes		
Aerobic work	30 minutes		
Integrated flexibility work			
Elastic cord work (light)			
8 exercises, 15 reps/exercise, 3 angles, 5 reps/angle		=	1,200
Light dumbbells (10 lbs)			
12 exercises, 9 reps/exercise, 3 angles, 3 reps/angle		=	900
Body work (feet elevated to tolerance)			
11 exercises, 15-20 reps/exercise, 3-4 angles,		=	19,800
5 reps/angle			
Machine work (to tolerance)			
9 exercises, 15-20 reps/exercise, 3-4 angles		=	10,100
5 reps/angle			
Heavy free-weight work (to tolerance)			
6 exercises, 15-20 reps/exercise, 3-4 angles,		=	0
5 reps/angle			

Total lbs   **32,000**

Day 6 (Friday)

Throwing work volumes

Bullpen warm-up and mound work =   20 pitches
No game

$$\text{Workload} = 20 \times 90 \text{ mph}^2 \times .01 \times \frac{1}{.88} = \textbf{1,841 ft-lbs}$$

Conditioning and resistance work volumes

Healthrider	5 minutes		
Aerobic work	5 minutes		
Integrated flexibility work to tolerance			
Elastic cord work (light)			
8 exercises, 15 reps/exercise, 3 angles, 5 reps/angle		=	1,200 (max)
Light dumbbells (weight to tolerance)			
12 exercises, 9 reps/exercise, 3 angles, 3 reps/angle		=	900
Body work (optional)		=	0
Machine work (optional)		=	0
No heavy free-weight work		=	0

Total lbs   **2,100**

Day 7 (Saturday)

Throwing work volumes

Bullpen warm-up mound work	=	20 pitches
Game 1 1/3 innings	=	20 pitches
	Total	40 pitches

$$\text{Workload} = 40 \times 90 \text{ mph}^2 \times .01 \times \frac{1}{.88} = \textbf{3,682 ft-lbs}$$

Conditioning and resistance work volumes

Healthrider	15 minutes	
Aerobic work	30 minutes	
Integrated flexibility work		
Elastic cord work (light)		
8 exercises, 15 reps/exercise, 3 angles, 5 reps/angle	=	1,200
Light dumbbells (5 lbs)		
12 exercises, 15 reps/exercise, 3 angles, 5 reps/angle	=	900
Body work (feet elevated to tolerance)		
11 exercises, 15-20 reps/exercise, 3-4 angles,	=	19,800
5 reps/angle		
Machine work (optional)	=	0
No heavy free weights	=	0
	Total lbs	**21,900**

Seven-Day Workload Totals

Our theoretical reliever's conditioning workloads and throwing workloads are less than those of our theoretical starter in the same time frame—a concession to the volume-frequency relationship of their roles on the pitching staff *and* cross-specific training. But as with starters, low-risk body work accounts for the large conditioning volume numbers.

Day	Conditioning volume	Throwing volume
Sunday	32,000	5,062
Monday	21,900	3,221
Tuesday	2,100	0
Wednesday	21,900	6,903
Thursday	32,000	0
Friday	2,100	1,841
Saturday	21,900	3,682
Totals:	133,900 lbs	20,709 lbs

Training Summary

Now you have examples of complete programs followed by a theoretical power starter and a setup power reliever. The micro cycle integrates all the information in chapters 1 through 7 and is a flexible routine for proper preparation to pitch. It is cross-specific, everything has a purpose, and choices within the program can solve most any conditioning problem or throwing difficulty. Protocols are logical in purpose, user-friendly, to tolerance, and have enough variety to avoid monotonous overtraining. Everything in this pitcher's pregame micro cycle is functional for the health and competitive success of his season's macro cycle. He is indeed fit to pitch.

The appendix for this book has a worksheet that you can use to map out a micro cycle for yourself. When you match the total program —strength training workloads with mound throwing and pitching training workloads—you have done everything the orthopedic community, the physical therapy community, and the baseball community can prescribe for a protocol to optimize physical talent and mechanical skill.

Part III

Fit to Pitch
Rehab and Nutrition

It's an unfortunate reality in baseball that players get hurt. In fact, I'd be willing to bet that every coach, parent, and athlete reading this book has had some experience with injury.

The good news, however, is that sports medicine and sport technology have greatly improved an athlete's chances of recovering from injury. In the past most injuries were career threatening—trick knees and thrown-out arms sent you home. Today, it's commonplace for joints and limbs to be surgically repaired—Tommy John's elbow and Orel Hershiser's shoulder are major-league proof positive.

165

But while the sports medicine and sport technology environ- ment gets better and better, there's still a gap between when a physical therapist or trainer declares a player "ready" and when he's "game ready" to compete at 100 percent capacity. This gap occurs because physical therapists are not coaches and coaches are not physical therapists. In the sequencing of medical rehab to physical therapy rehab there should be a performance rehab before a player accesses coaching for competition.

This is the baseline for part III: fit to pitch rehab and nutrition. Chapters 10 and 11 address performance rehab so coaches and players can feel more confident about what it takes to regain competitive form after an injury *and* minimize the chances of reinjury.

Chapter

10

Rehabilitative Training

"Doc, it hurts when I do this."
"Well, don't do it!"

The Hee Haw variety show

What happens when a pitcher isn't fit to pitch—when he throws only with pain, when he is hurt and can't throw, when he is facing surgery, or when he has had an operation and is trying to recuperate? From the medical and coaching standpoint, you call this rehabilitation time. From the athlete's standpoint, you call this a neurophysical and psychoneuroimmunological nightmare. It is going from penthouse to outhouse with emotions, sense of self, and sense of purpose. A pitcher in rehab must work longer and smarter than he did to compete with none of the feedback provided by competition. Basically, it means overcoming fear and pain to build enough strength to work on the physical imbalances or mechanical flaws that caused the initial injury, all the while feeling the baseball world is passing him by. If you are saying to yourself that this rehab thing sounds more mental-emotional than physical-mechanical, you are exactly right! In fact, there is very little difference between *pre*hab physical-mechanical work and *re*hab physical-mechanical work.

Rehabilitation is taking the body to tolerance with lots of frequency and very low intensity while tissue repairs itself. Rehab work is also longer term work—a macro approach that must first repair an athlete's pathology before it prepares him for competition. Everything done in rehab is done in smaller increments over an increased time frame with the same performance absolutes: a functional integration of (1) mental conditioning, (2) nutritional conditioning, (3) physical conditioning, and (4) mechanical conditioning.

In this chapter I will share the things that have helped the recovery rate and the recovery time of injured players I have worked with in the U.S. and Japan. You will notice I prioritize the performance absolutes a little differently for rehab work because I've found mental-emotional toughness and a healthy blood chemistry must precede physical conditioning and skill training. It doesn't do any good to resistance train or instruct proper pitching mechanics if the player is physically incapable due to inappropriate dissonances about (1) perceived pain, (2) fear of pain, (3) fear of reinjury, and/or (4) fear of recovery. It's also a medical reality that players with poor blood chemistries (i.e., poor nutrition) heal slower and are more prone to reinjury during rehab.

Mental Conditioning

From a health psychology perspective, a rehab player must have firm boundaries, clear expectations, and many affirmations with goals that are realistic, achievable, and accomplished in a series of miniobjectives. These are baby steps toward being competitive. Every rehab athlete will have highs and lows, as well as plateaus (where it seems as if *nothing* is being accomplished positively or negatively). Coach, trainer, or athlete must never put results ahead of proper mechanics and must never be in a hurry. Time frames are irrelevant beyond knowing that you cannot push Mother Nature's healing process beyond the quality of your information, your optimal workload, and your genetics. I tell rehabbers they must think in macro cycles not micro cycles. Rehabilitation takes time—period!

What does a coach or player do mentally to handle being sidelined? Here are some suggestions that have worked for me, in the professional environment and in the collegiate and high school ranks.

Mental Training Tips for Pros

There is a *lot* of pressure to rehab quickly in the pros. A season lost to injury can hurt not only a team's record, but also a pitcher's advancement to the next level or his pocketbook. It's important, then, that players try to block out the extra worries and focus on getting better. These strategies have worked for me.

• Use the buddy system whenever possible. If each hurt player has a body-work buddy for daily training, it helps his attitude and motivation and spreads out the fear and frustration factors.

• Give an identity to your rehab group. I called my guys the "MASH Unit" when I worked rehabilitation for the Texas Rangers. Why the special identity? Because injured players seldom feel a part of the real team. It is a given that healthy players must get first priority from coaches and trainers because they are competing. Initially, this is hard on an injured player's attitude. So create an atmosphere of teamwork around getting healthy.

• As soon as possible, and wherever feasible, I integrate rehabbers back into workouts with their healthy teammates. Doing some of the same work as healthy players both helps the rehabbing athletes and promotes the team concept.

- I also had the healthier rehabbers work with the incoming "bent and broken." It seemed to help keep the veterans more focused and give a bit of encouragement to newer rehab athletes. They got information from someone going through the ordeal, not just from a coach who could only talk about it. This really worked well for the Rangers. Imagine having a big leaguer like Mike Scioscia or Bruce Hurst working alongside an "A" ballplayer like Dave Chavarria or David Manning.

- Finally, when a rehab player graduated from the disability list to team assignment, we had a MASH Unit "we're behind you" send-off dinner to finish rehabilitation on a positive note.

Mental Training for High School and College Rehabbers

Unfortunately, in an amateur setting, the coach and trainer do not have the same working format as the pros. However, the same squad identification, buddy work, and team integration principles can work. Have rehab players buddy up (even if it is with a nonplayer). When the injured player is able, get him back into teamwork. Have him lead flexibility training. (He'll push the healthy players—watch!) Have him help with soft toss, coaching first base, charting pitches, scouting other teams—whatever! Keep him involved! Rehab doesn't have to be mental and emotional isolation.

Nutritional Conditioning

Rehabilitation is wound healing. Wounds heal quicker with proper blood chemistry. Proper blood chemistry comes from proper nutrition. If pitchers aren't eating right on their own, then it's time for the coaching staff to see that they do. We'll discuss nutrition in detail in chapter 11.

Rehabilitative Training   171

Physical Conditioning

I have already mentioned that rehabilitation protocols are *exactly* the same as prehabilitation protocols except for working to tolerance at very low intensity with a lot of frequency. There is something new, however, for players having surgery. The more functionally strong and aerobically fit an athlete is *before* an operation, the quicker will be his rehabilitation *after* the operation. So don't give up functional fitness just because you are having surgery. But remember, no athlete should throw, swing, run, or catch unless he is functionally fit to do so.

Mechanical Conditioning

My checkpoints for throwing skills, in rehab, are all done on flat ground. Reread chapter 6 if you need to. In rehab, a throwing endurance base must be built while relearning the proper skills of pitching.

I have found a rule of 100 that seems to be a good litmus test for determining if a pitcher has the strength and endurance to start mound skill work:

100 long-toss one-hops at 100+ feet and 100% intensity with no stiffness or pain = mound work ready

Rehab Summary

That is rehab training. The different sequencing of performance absolutes—(1) mental and emotional conditioning, (2) nutritional conditioning, (3) physical conditioning, and (4) mechanical conditioning—plus working at lower intensity with more frequency are the only nuances involved.

Chapter

11

The Pitcher's Training Table

Some people eat to live. Some people live to eat. Athletes eat to compete.

Dr. Dick Cloonan, oral surgeon, sports nutritionist, San Diego Padres

After working with athletes and their diets for 15 years, I have come to a significant conclusion about eating habits: people eat the way their mothers fed them. So, when you try to change a player's diet, you are subconsciously fighting a whole lot of Mom's nurturing. And, no matter how good the athlete's conscious intentions, his mom is always going to win the subconscious food fight.

The "To Do" and "Try To" of Nutrition

In working with pitchers and nutrition, I use a philosophy that "you can't push a rope so pull it instead." I remind them that nutrition is *not* dieting. It is blood chemistry and stabilizing metabolism to balance daily energy needs for repairing, preparing, and competing. Metabolism works best when it is working, so your pitchers should start eating three to five small meals a day with proper nutritional intake and proper timing as a function of three variables:

1. Food combining. Meals should be either protein oriented or complex-carbohydrate oriented, in combination with fruits/vegetables. The best time for protein is after a high-energy time of day. The best time for complex carbohydrates is before a high-energy time of day. Keep liquid intake to 12 ounces during the meal, so digestive enzymes aren't diluted.

2. Food rotating. Players can eat the foods they like best, but should try not to eat the same food type prepared the same way twice in 72 hours (three days). This helps blood chemistry by reducing food sensitivity problems.

3. Food supplementing. Your pitchers should take these supplements in the middle of their largest meal so food chemistry can interact with vitamin chemistry. Supplements should never be taken on an empty stomach.

- Megavitamin—any variety.
- Digestive enzyme—We are an enzyme-deficient society.
- Chromium picolinate—a fat burner for fat storage problems only.

Any or all of the following antioxidants will combat and neutralize free radicals in the body. Free radicals are harmful little molecules roaming around the bloodstream—the net result of stress and distress in daily living.

- Vitamin C
- Vitamin E
- Beta carotene
- Selenium
- CoQ10
- Pychnogynol
- Lycopene

With these three variables as a "to do" foundation, advise your pitchers of these "try tos":

Avoid:

- Fat grams. Remember that nerves don't work in fat and stored fat takes four times the energy to move around than lean muscle.

- Refined carbohydrates. These make your blood sugar go nuclear. They have very little nutritional value and are stored unused as fat.

- Empty calories. The body wastes more energy metabolizing these than it gets from the food itself. Again, the unused empty calories are stored as fat.

- Alcohol. Remember, your body is wound healing. Alcohol is a diuretic and thus depletes body fluids. It also takes oxygen out of the bloodstream and thins the blood of nutrients that rebuild tissue. Finally, it produces empty calories that get stored as fat.

- Nicotine. Skill is neuromuscular memory. Nicotine affects skill and perception by altering nerve synapses. It is a vasoconstrictor that makes it harder to get oxygen to muscle tissue, so the heart is forced to work overtime. Also, all tobacco is carcinogenic, and smokeless tobacco contains sugar.

- Soft drinks. These are composed of empty calories, refined carbohydrates, caffeine, and salt, all of which adversely affect metabolism.

- Fried food. Fat! Fat! Fat!

- Eating large meals late at night. This forces the heart to pump blood to the stomach and digestive tract instead of relaxing and flushing the bodily systems while you sleep.

<u>Choose:</u>

- Fresh fruit and vegetables. These foods are best raw for natural roughage and digestive enzymes.
- Low-fat and no-fat alternatives (whenever possible).
- Home cooking over restaurant food over fast food (in that order, whenever possible).
- Breakfast! Eating a good breakfast sets the tone of the whole day. It starts your metabolic engine and stabilizes blood sugar.
- Light snacks between lunch and dinner, and between dinner and bed. This keeps the metabolic engine running, minimizing fat storage.

A Two-Week Training Menu

I am always looking for smart eating tips, menus, and guides. The smartest I have found is this two-week menu. It represents efficient combination and rotation of foods. All it requires is that your pitchers take food supplements during their big meals, eat additional complex carbohydrates before workouts and games, eat additional protein after workouts and games, and, to accomplish our food rotation goal, alternate a food type *within* the meal wherever you see "same as day X."

A 14-Day Training Menu*

Day 1

Breakfast:
1 cup dry cereal, oatmeal, or oat bran
1 cup skim milk

*Note. This is the Hilton Head Metabolism Diet adapted by permission from the book of that name by Dr. Peter M. Miller and published by Warner Books, 1984.

1 banana

1/2 cup orange juice

1 slice whole wheat toast with 1 teaspoon low-sugar jelly

Morning Snack:

1 orange

Lunch:

Tuna-salad sandwich (1/3 cup tuna packed in water with 1 tablespoon nonfat mayonnaise, 2 slices whole wheat bread, tomato, and lettuce)

Afternoon Snack:

1 low-fat muffin

Dinner:

Catalina chicken

1 cup mixed stir-fried vegetables (lightly sautéed, using vegetable spray)

Evening Snack:

Celery and carrot sticks with nonfat peppercorn ranch dressing or creamy nonfat dressing of your choice

Day 2

Breakfast:

3 slices French toast made with low-calorie wheat or white bread, 3 egg whites, and skim milk

3 tablespoons low-calorie maple syrup

1 orange

Morning Snack:

8 ounces nonfat yogurt with fruit

Lunch:

Pita bread stuffed with 1 tablespoon tuna packed in water, 1/4 cup diced onion, 1 diced tomato, 1 cup shredded lettuce

Dinner:
Eggplant Parmesan
Small tossed salad with 2 tablespoons nonfat Italian dressing and 1 teaspoon Parmesan cheese
1 hard roll with 1 teaspoon fat-free margarine

Day 3

Breakfast:
Same as day 1

Lunch:
Primavera salad
2 slices melba toast

Afternoon Snack:
1/2 medium cantaloupe

Dinner:
5 ounces broiled or baked white fish (such as sole, flounder, grouper, or catfish)
1/2 cup low-fat yogurt gently warmed with 1 tablespoon Dijon mustard as sauce
1 baked potato with 2 tablespoons nonfat sour cream
1 cup steamed broccoli or carrots

Evening Snack:
1 low-fat oat bran muffin or 2 low-fat cookies (100 calories total)

Day 4

Breakfast:
1 oat bran English muffin with 1 tablespoon low-sugar jelly
1/4 cantaloupe
1 cup skim milk

Lunch:

Large tossed salad (2 cups romaine lettuce; 1 diced tomato; 1/2 cup diced cucumber; 1 diced carrot; small sliced onion; 1/4 cup chickpeas; 2 ounces diced chicken, turkey, or tofu; 2 teaspoons Parmesan cheese; 2 tablespoons nonfat dressing)

2 slices melba toast

1/4 cantaloupe

Afternoon Snack:

8 ounces nonfat yogurt and fruit

Dinner:

Shrimp scampi

1 cup brown rice

6-8 steamed asparagus spears or 1 cup green vegetable of your choice

Day 5

Breakfast:
Same as day 2

Lunch:
Shrimp and macaroni salad

1 apple or pear

Afternoon Snack:
1 low-fat oat bran muffin or 2 low-fat cookies (100 calories total)

Dinner:
1 cup chili

5 nonfat crackers

Day 6

Breakfast:
Same as day 1

Lunch:
1 cup low-fat canned vegetable or bean soup

5 nonfat crackers

Chicken salad sandwich (2 ounces diced cooked chicken breast, 1 tablespoon nonfat mayonnaise, 2 slices whole wheat bread, lettuce, and tomato slices)

Afternoon Snack:
1 orange

Dinner:
Spaghetti (1 1/2 cups cooked spaghetti with 1/4 cup low-fat tomato sauce and 2 tablespoons Parmesan cheese)

1 dinner roll

Small salad with nonfat dressing

Day 7

Breakfast:
1 poached egg

1 cup low-fat hash browns (use microwaved baked potato, diced and mixed with 1/4 cup sautéed onion)

1/2 grapefruit

2 slices whole wheat toast with 2 teaspoons fat-free margarine

1/2 cup orange juice

Lunch:
Tossed salad (see day 4)

1 cup chicken noodle soup

5 nonfat crackers

Afternoon Snack:
1/4 honeydew or other melon

Dinner:
4-ounce broiled pork tenderloin topped with 1 1/2 teaspoons commercial barbecue sauce

1 cup mashed potatoes

1 cup steamed vegetables

1 whole wheat roll with 1 teaspoon fat-free margarine

Evening Snack:
1 fruit of your choice

Day 8

Breakfast:
Same as day 1

Lunch:
Turkey sandwich (2 ounces turkey, 2 slices whole wheat
bread, 1 tablespoon nonfat mayonnaise, tomato slices,
lettuce)

Celery and carrot sticks

Dinner:
5 ounces white fish (such as flounder, sole, grouper, or
catfish) baked in juice of 1 lemon

1 baked potato with 2 tablespoons nonfat sour cream

6-8 spears steamed asparagus or 1 cup green vegetable of
your choice

1 dinner roll with 1 teaspoon diet margarine

Evening Snack:
1/2 cantaloupe or 1 orange

Day 9

Breakfast:
Same as day 1

Lunch:
American sub
Small tossed salad with 2 tablespoons nonfat dressing

Afternoon Snack:
Choice of 1 fruit

Dinner:
Chicken enchilada
10 low-fat tortilla chips
1/4 cup salsa
1/2 cup brown rice

Evening Snack:
2 cups raw vegetables with 1/4 cup creamy nonfat dressing
as a dip

Day 10

Breakfast:
Same as day 1

Lunch:
Spinach salad (2 cups fresh spinach, 2 teaspoons bacon bits, 1 hard-boiled egg, 1/2 cup sliced mushrooms, 1 tablespoon diced onion, 2 tablespoons nonfat dressing)
2 slices melba toast
1/4 cantaloupe

Afternoon Snack:
1 apple

Dinner:
4-ounce skinned, floured turkey breast sautéed in 2 teaspoons margarine and juice of 1 lemon

1/2 cup egg noodles with 1 tablespoon Parmesan cheese,
1/2 teaspoon diet margarine

1 cup steamed zucchini

1 dinner roll

Evening Snack:
1 orange

Day 11

Breakfast:
Same as day 1

Lunch:
Tuna-salad sandwich (see day 1)

Carrot and celery sticks

Afternoon Snack:
1 1/2 cups seedless grapes

Dinner:
Shrimp scampi

1 cup brown rice

1/2 cup peas

1/2 cup carrots

Evening Snack:
Choice of 1 fruit

Day 12

Breakfast:
Same as day 1

Lunch:
Primavera salad
2 slices melba toast

Dinner:
1 baked 16-ounce Cornish game hen
1 cup brown rice
1 cup steamed broccoli florets
1 hard roll

Evening Snack:
Choice of 1 fruit

Day 13

Breakfast:
Same as day 1

Lunch:
1 cup canned mixed beans (drained and rinsed) mixed with 1/4 cup each chopped red pepper, onion, tomato, and 1 1/2 teaspoons low-cal Italian dressing
1 slice melba toast
1 apple

Afternoon Snack:
1 low-fat oat bran muffin or 2 low-fat cookies (100 calories total)

Dinner:
Fettuccine Alfredo
Small tossed salad with 2 tablespoons nonfat dressing
1 hard roll

Evening Snack:
1 cup strawberries with 1/4 cup nonfat vanilla yogurt

Day 14

Breakfast:
Same as day 7

Lunch:
Pita bread with 1 ounce tuna packed in water, 1/4 cup diced onion, 1 diced tomato
1 cup shredded lettuce
2 tablespoons nonfat dressing

Afternoon Snack:
Choice of 1 fruit

Dinner:
8-ounce broiled lobster tail
1 1/2 tablespoons diet margarine
1 ear corn or 1/2 cup other seasonal white vegetable
1 cup steamed broccoli
1 baked potato
1 dinner roll

Evening Snack:
Choice of 1 fruit

Integrating Metabolism and Blood Chemistry With Your Training

Now that you have some nutritional philosophy, strategies about how and what to eat and not eat, and a hypothetical two-week menu, let's put some numbers to it all. The following pages will show how metabolism and blood chemistry can be integrated with macro-cycle rehab repairing and preparing to compete as well as with macro- and micro-cycle prehab repairing, preparing, and competing. Resistance training, skill training, competing, and recovery cycles will all be more efficient. Nutrition is another piece of the fit-to-pitch puzzle.

The rest of this chapter will focus mostly on blood sugar and protein. Blood sugar, metabolizing with oxygen, is the body's primary resource for energy in all physical activity. It's only logical to identify the best food sources for this resource requirement if an athlete wants to properly fuel for training and competing. Protein is the body's primary resource for wound healing and tissue building. Eating the best food sources for efficient protein intake will enhance repairing and preparing for competition. Finally, knowing *when* to eat— thereby influencing the timing and amount of blood sugar and protein available to the body in the macro and/or micro cycle— is equally important to repairing, preparing, and competing.

Complex Carbohydrates and Blood Sugar

Which causes the greater blood-sugar spike, a bagel or a cup of yogurt? The answer may surprise you. David Jenkins, MD, PhD, of the University of Toronto, measured the "glycemic index" of selected foods and their corresponding effects on blood sugar (or glucose) levels. Figure 11.1 shows the percentage rise in blood-sugar levels after subjects were given food portions of equal carbohydrate loads. Starchy foods like potatoes rate high because they are made of long molecule chains of glucose that quickly enter the bloodstream. (Table sugar is only half glucose, which accounts for its relatively low rating.) Foods that are easily digested tend to have higher ratings than those that break down more slowly. Fat content slows sugar absorption; thus ice cream, which contains butterfat, has a lower rating than shredded wheat.

Try to maintain a steady rate of sugar inflow and avoid the surge and crash cycle of fast carbs; when blood sugar plummets after a sharp rise, hunger and fatigue inevitably follow. Slow-burning complex carbohydrates such as beans and lentils (rich in protein and vitamins) should be a component of any weight-reduction strategy. If, however, you feel the need to indulge in fast-burning carbohydrates, make sure to balance them with slow-burn carbs.

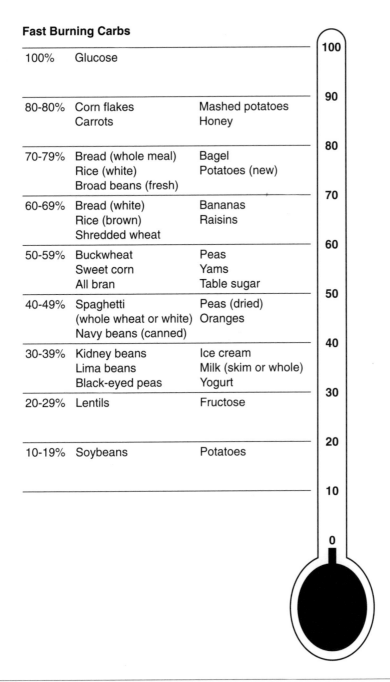

Figure 11.1   Percentage rise in blood sugar after ingestion of diverse foods.
*Note. Data provided by Dr. David Jenkins, MD in R. Arnot, 1995, "The New Paradigms," *Men's Journal* February/1995: 75.

Protein for Pitching

Protein satisfies your appetite more efficiently than carbs or fat because it takes longer to digest. So, by including small amounts of protein in your meals and snacks, you can cut down on the amount of food and calories you eat. The trick is to plan your protein intake. You may choose to get most of your protein in the morning before you exercise. Another effective strategy is to take in protein after exercise when your body is repairing tissue and muscle.

Protein Providers

Five to 10 percent of the energy demand of an athlete engaged in intense exercise can be supplied by protein. Look for proteins in the following sources:

- Eggs
- Skim milk
- Whole milk and cheese
- Fish
- Lean red meat, turkey, and chicken
- Corn
- Rice

When you go for protein go for high quality; the proteins listed above build muscle better than others. Remember, though, to differentiate between quality and quantity. Many high protein foods are also high fat. You want foods with high protein but lower fat. Skim milk, baked fish, and rice are among your best bets. High quality protein can also be found in wheat, oatmeal, peanut butter, and soy flour.

Getting the Right Amount

The USDA recommends 0.4 grams of protein per pound of body weight eacy day. But, you've got to remember that the USDA makes its recommendations for the largely sedentary US adult population. Athletes need more, as delineated in Table 11.1

Table 11.1 Grams of Protein per Pound of Body Weight for Athletes	
Competitive athlete, adult	0.6-0.9
Growing teenage athlete	0.9-1.0
Adult building muscle mass	0.7-0.9
Athlete restricting calories	0.8-1.0

Adapted, by permission, from N. Clark, 1996, *Nancy Clark's Sports Nutrition Guidebook*, 2nd ed. (Champaign, IL: Human Kinetics).

How do you figure out your proper daily protein intake? It's a two-step process.

First, check Table 11.1 to see where you fit. Let's assume that you're a 140-pound junior starting for your high school team. You'd identify yourself as a "growing teenage athlete" and figure your protein intake range as follows:

140 lb × 0.9 g/lb = 126 g protein

140 lb × 1.0 g/lb = 140 g protein

Thus, each day you'd need 126 and 140 grams of protein in your diet.

Second, track your daily intake. List everything you eat and drink for a day. Use the nutrition information on food labels to keep a running tab of how you're doing. Be sure to consider how many servings you're eating. For example, a can of tuna may have 15 grams protein per serving. But, look closely at the nutrition information on the can and you may find that the little can you're holding is (incredibly enough) two servings. So, if you eat the whole thing, you're getting 30 grams of protein.

Table 11.2 lists the amount of protein in some common foods that may not have nutritional information on their labels.

Table 11.2 Protein Amounts for Common Foods

Food	Amount	Grams of Protein
Almonds	12 nuts	3
McDonald's Big Mac	1	24.6
Cheddar cheese	1 oz	30
Chicken breast	4 oz roasted	35
Cod	3 oz (baked)	19.4
Egg	1	6
Egg white	from 1 egg	3.5
Flounder	3.5 oz (baked)	30
Hamburger	4 oz (broiled)	30
Pork loin	4 oz (roasted)	30
Round steak	3.5 oz (broiled)	31.7
Tofu (extra firm)	3.5 oz	11

Data from N. Clark, 1996, *Nancy Clark's Sports Nutrition Guidebook*, 2nd ed. (Champaign, IL: Human Kinetics) and, R. Arnot, 1995, *Dr. Bob Arnot's Guide to Turning Back the Clock* (Boston: Little, Brown and Company), 53-54.

Most fruits and vegetables have only small amounts of protein that may contribute a total of 5 to 10 grams of protein per day, depending on how much you eat. Butter, margarine, oil, sugar, candy, soda, alcohol, and coffee contain no protein, and desserts contain very little.

Remember to figure out how much protein you need. Read labels to monitor your intake. And pick quality protein—usually foods that have a high amount of protein per calorie. Armed with this information, you can now adjust your diet to get the protein you need to build muscle and reach your pitching potential.

Nutrition Summary

Nobody is perfect with their nutrition. Your personal goal is up to you. My challenge is that you do more right eating than wrong eating. The "supplement salad" I suggested is an insurance policy for short-term lapses, not a fail-safe solution for a long-term total lapse. Remember our Betty Crocker analogy—even Betty burns a cake once in a while, but day in and day out, she is a pretty good cook! If you're satisfied with your energy level and how it matches up with your workout and competition regimen, your nutrition is probably fine (you have balanced blood chemistry). If, however, you're 1) chronically tired, 2) gaining unwanted weight even though working hard, 3) taking too long to bounce back from training and competing, 4) having trouble concentrating, or 5) unable to control your emotions, poor nutrition is probably the culprit.

Appendix

Weekly Resistance and Mound-Throwing Volume Worksheet

Resistance-training volumes (upper body)

Elastic cord. 8 exercises; 1 set, 15 reps each with high, medium, and low tension cords; to tolerance. _____

Light dumbbells. 12 exercises; 1 set, 3 angles, 5 reps at each angle; with 3- to 10-lb dumbbells. _____

Body work. 8 exercises; 1 set, 3 or 4 angles, 5 reps at each angle.

For horizontal work, lift your body weight ×

- 0.6 when feet are below center of gravity
- 0.8 when feet are level with center of gravity
- 1.0 when feet are above center of gravity

For vertical work, lift your body weight × 1.0 at all times _____

Machine work. 5 machines, 1 set, 3 or 4 angles, 5 reps at each angle, with resistance to tolerance facing forward. _____

Example:
1 machine (pec deck), 1 set, 3 angles with forearms stable, 5 reps at each angle. 1 set, 3 angles with forearms moving, 5 reps at each angle. Resistance to tolerance facing backward. _____

Free weights. 6 exercises, 1 set, 2 to 4 postures, 3 to 4 angles, 5 reps each with resistance to tolerance. Bench press 1 set, 15 reps to tolerance. _____

TOTAL WEEKLY TRAINING VOLUME ══════

Mound-throwing volumes (upper body)

$$\text{Number of pitches} \times (\text{velocity})^2 \times .01 \times \frac{1}{\text{mechanical efficiency}} = $$ ══════

193

Index

About the Author

Tom House is recognized as one of the world's foremost authorities on pitching. In the Major Leagues from 1967 to 1979, he pitched for the Atlanta Braves, Boston Red Sox, and Seattle Mariners. He has coached major league pitchers since 1980 for the Houston Astros, Texas Rangers, and San Diego Padres. He also has coached in Tokyo and Latin America.

Another dimension of Tom's expertise is as scientist and researcher. His company, BioKinetics, is a leader in computerized, three-dimensional motion analysis, which helps athletes learn to maximize performance through proper biomechanics.

Assistant to the general manager and international baseball consultant for the San Diego Padres, Tom also travels the world as a consultant, lecturer, and sports psychologist for many professional and amateur baseball players. He has appeared as a guest psychologist on both *60 Minutes* and *Geraldo.* And he appears nationally on television infomercials for HealthRider.

Tom, who holds a PhD in psychology, is author of six previous books on baseball and coauthor of four others and has filmed seven videos, including his highly successful *The Pitching Edge.* He is a member of the Major League Baseball Players' Association, the American College of Sports Medicine, and the Association for the Advancement of Applied Sport Psychology.

Tom lives in Del Mar, California, and enjoys jogging, fitness activities, and golf.

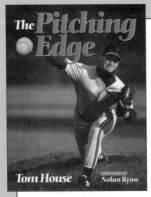

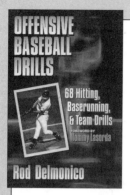
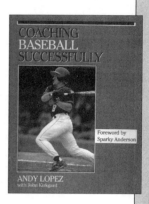
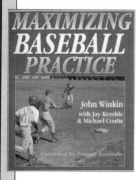